Every Body Has Parasites

If You're Alive, You're at Risk!

VALERIE SAXION

Strength
& Honor

BRONZE BOW PUBLISHING
www.bronzebowpublishing.com

The information in this book is for educational purposes only and is not recommended as a means of diagnosing or treating an illness. Neither the publisher nor author is engaged in rendering professional advice or services to the individual reader. All matters regarding physical and mental health should be supervised by a health practitioner knowledgeable in treating that particular condition. Neither the author nor the publisher shall be liable or responsible for any loss, injury, or damage allegedly arising from any information or suggestion in this book.

CONTENTS

DEDICATION

JESUS SAID,

*"There is no greater gift than
to lay down your life for your friend."
I want to thank those friends
who lay down their lives daily
to support me in my work
and who have also contributed
in the preparation of this book.*

*Melissa Madeley, Cortney Caylor,
Karen Haskell, Lora McDaniel,
Rachel Meldonado, Lynn Alston,
and Donna Spaulding.
I love you all.*

ABOUT THE AUTHOR

DR. VALERIE SAXION IS ONE OF AMERICA'S MOST ARTICULATE CHAMPIONS OF NUTRITION AND SPIRITUAL HEALING. A twenty-year veteran of health science with a primary focus in naturopathy, Valerie has a delightful communication style and charming demeanor that will open your heart, clear your mind, and uplift you to discover abundant natural health God's way. Her pearls of wisdom and life-saving advice are critical for success and survival in today's toxic world.

As the co-founder of Valerie Saxion's Silver Creek Labs, a premier manufacturer and distributor of nutritional supplements and health products that cover a wide range of healing modalities, Dr. Saxion has seen firsthand the power of God's remedies as the sick are healed and the lame walk. "It's what I love most about what God has called me to do," she says.

Valerie Saxion is the host of TBN's *On Call*, which airs twice weekly across America. The program is dedicated to bringing the most up-to-date health and nutritional information to the viewing audience. Dr. Saxion is one of TBN's favorite speakers and can be seen quarterly on the flagship show, *Praise the Lord.* The audience is nationwide as well as international, with a potential 33 million broadcast households.

She is also seen on the Daystar Television Network and Cornerstone Television Network. Dr. Saxion has been interviewed on numerous radio talk shows as well as television appearances nationwide and in Canada. Hosts love to open the line for callers to phone in their health concerns while Dr. Saxion gives on-the-air advice and instruction.

She has also lectured at scores of health events nationwide and in Canada. She has advised international government leaders, professional athletes, television personalities, and the lady next door. "All with the same great results," she says, "if they will only follow the recommendations."

After attending one of Dr. Saxion's lectures, you may have cried, you may have laughed, you may get insight, but one thing is sure: You will leave empowered with the tools to live and love in a healthy body!

Dr. Saxion is also the author of *How to Feel Great All the Time* as well as four very practical, life-changing booklets, including *How to Stop Candida and Other Yeast Conditions in Their Tracks, The Easy Way to Regain and Maintain Your Perfect Weight, Conquering the Fatigue, Depression and Weight Gain Caused by Low Thyroid,* and *How to Detoxify and Renew*

Your Body From Within. She is currently a monthly colum-nist for BeautyWalk.com, hosted by Peter Lamas, famous makeup artist and hair designer for the rich and famous.

Married to Jim Saxion for twenty-plus years, they are the parents of eight healthy children, ages toddler to 21.

To schedule Dr. Saxion for a lecture or interview, please contact Joy at 1-800-493-1146, or fax 817-236-5411, or email at valeriesaxon@cs.com.

Perhaps you are unfamiliar with the meaning of a natur-opath, or N.D. Michael Murray, who is probably the most well-known naturopath in the field, defines it in these terms:

"At the forefront of the natural medicine movement is naturopathy, a method of healing that employs various nat-ural means to empower an individual to achieve health. In addition to providing recommendations on life-style, diet, and exercise, naturopathic physicians may elect to utilize a variety of natural healing techniques, including clinical nutrition, herbal medicine, homeopathy, Oriental medicine and acupuncture, hydrotherapy, physical medicine, includ-ing massage and therapeutic manipulation and counseling.

"The modern naturopathic physician provides all phases of primary health care. He or she is trained to be the doctor first seen by the patient for general (non-emer-gency) health care. Some naturopathic physicians choose to emphasize a particular healing technique, while others are more eclectic and utilize a number of techniques. Some naturopaths elect to specialize in particular medical fields, such as pediatrics, natural childbirth, and physical medicine.

"Although the terms naturopathy and naturopathic medicine were not used until the late nineteenth century, their roots go back thousands of years. Drawing from the healing wisdom of many cultures, including India (Ayurvedic), China (Taoist), and Greece (Hippocratic), naturopathic medicine is a system of medicine founded on the four time-tested medical principles—Naturopath, N.D.; Medical Doctor, M.D.; Osteopath, D.O.; and Chiropractor, D.C."

Dr. Saxion is a practicing Christian and does not adhere to occult practices or Eastern religions.

INTRODUCTION

REGARDLESS OF HOW YOU HAVE COME INTO POSSESSION OF THIS BOOK, I promise you that *it is for you*. I realize that's a big promise, but the odds are heavily weighted in my favor, especially if you live in the United States. Dr. Frank Nova, Chief of the Laboratory for Parasitic Disease of the prestigious National Institute of Health said, "In terms of numbers, there are more parasitic infections acquired in this country than Africa."

By the time you finish reading this book, and many people won't put it down until they're at the end, you will not be able to deny that its message is for you. Many outstanding doctors in the United States believe that 80 to 90 percent of the American public has parasites. My own in-house studies suggest 100 percent, although it's taken years of working in the health and nutrition field to convince me of this.

As you might imagine, as a naturopathic doctor, I am consumed with healthy living. The medical establishment has even come up with a relatively new name for those of us who are extremely enthusiastic with health, and if you are also a passionately health-conscious person, you might find this same label in your health records: "Orthorexia Nervosa." It is a term that describes a concern with eating healthily that becomes an obsession and a hindrance from enjoying a normal life. As of the writing of this book, I'm certain that this label will be fixed upon me even stronger, but based upon what I know to be true my purpose is to make you very conscious of the foods you allow in your home as well as the way those foods are prepared. It need not turn into an obsession or a nightmare, but the reality of parasites must be considered if we want to live healthy, fulfilled lives.

I have a husband of 23 years and eight healthy children, ranging from a toddler to a daughter in her mid twenties. Beginning with my first child and with all the children who have followed, Jim and I diligently monitored the food that entered their bodies. We eat well, we love our foods, but we are very careful that it's the right food and in the right amounts. So imagine my surprise as our whole family— Jim and I and each of the children—was first introduced to parasite cleansing and we came up with positive results. One hundred percent positive results! I could understand that the kids probably ate a mud pie or kissed the dog at some point in time that brought them into contact with parasites, and I know that my husband will sneak a hotdog now and then. But what about me? When I passed the first roundworm and liver flukes, I realized all the reports I had studied were factual! Even I was a host.

Then I asked my office staff to take part in this parasite cleanse as well, and 100 percent of those who did reported passing parasites. We've even kept some of the specimens for doubters. The fact that we're shocked by the hard evidence, or disgusted with the ugliness of it all, doesn't change the reality of our condition.

When Copernicus concluded 500 years ago that the earth was *not* the center of the universe, but was in fact hurtling through space in a yearly orbit around the sun, how do you think his revolutionary theory was received by the scholars of his day? Do you imagine they embraced him? No. In fact, he was scoffed at and the subject of ridicule, despite the scientific evidence he had.

My point is this: In life, as in history, what's *right* and what's accepted by the mainstream are rarely one and the same. When it comes to this subject, despite the fact that you may hear little about parasites from mainstream health professionals, many other professionals acknowledge that the problem does exists, and some of them see it for what it really is, a crisis, and they deal with it that way.

Dr. Ross Anderson says, "I believe the single most undiagnosed health challenge in the history of the human race is parasites. I realize that is a pretty brave statement, but it is based on my 20 years of experience, with more than 20,000 patients."

Anne Louis Gittleman is a nutritionist and international lecturer who has written the book, *Guess What Came to Dinner? Parasites and Your Health.* She has this to say: "You may be the unsuspecting victim of the parasite epidemic that is affecting millions of Americans. It is an epidemic that knows no territorial, economic, or sexual boundaries. It is a silent epidemic of which most doctors in this country are not even aware."

My purpose in writing this book is to help thousands of people come to understand this truth, and it has become a passion for me. When I realized that *Every Body* had a need where I could make a difference, I knew this was something God had made me accountable for. Just because we don't live in a Third World country and our sanitization methods are advanced has not stopped parasites from being a formidable though often hidden problem. It is a lot easier to become a parasitic host than you think, and you're about to find out some of the ways they infect us.

By reading *Every Body Has Parasites,* you will see that "if you're alive, you're at risk." And acting as your own health advisor for a while, you've put yourself years ahead of the pack, much like Copernicus was in his day.

PARASITES 101

IN THE SPRING OF 1993, THE NATIONAL INSTITUTE OF ALLERGY AND INFECTIOUS DISEASE reported 100 deaths and more than 400,000 people having fallen ill from the parasite *cryptosporidium*, a protozoan (a one-celled organism) that had infected an entire city's water system. And in what city did the water supply contamination take place? Calcutta? Bangkok? Or perhaps Mogadishu?

No. The parasitic infection occurred in Milwaukee, Wisconsin. Over a year later, in October 1994, NBC's *Dateline* reported *cryptosporidium* as the cause of deaths and illnesses in New York City. That was followed in September 1998 by the same parasite causing widespread water contamination in Sydney, Australia. One does not need to travel to a poor Third World country or trek deep into the tropics to find parasites doing their damage on the insides of human lives.

If you were in the Pacific Northwest in 1993, you will recall the deeply feared *E. coli* bacteria outbreak in which 477 people were infected and two children died from contaminated, undercooked hamburger. In 1994, 11 more people were infected in Washington State from contaminated ground beef, and also in 1994, 15 people were infected from contaminated salami. Additional *E. coli* bacteria outbreaks have occurred in the United States from non-beef sources, including lettuce and salad bars where foods were contaminated by improperly cleaned utensils, working surfaces, and infected food handlers. In addition, outbreaks have occurred in people who have consumed garden vegetables fertilized with animal manure, unpasteurized apple cider, and homemade venison jerky.

Parasitic experts estimate that there are between 100 to 130 common parasites being hosted in the American populace today. They vary from a microscopic amoeba that destroys the lining of the intestines of human beings and produces the painful disease called amoebic dysentery to several feet-long tapeworms that are the stuff of our most horrific nightmares. For most of us, just the thought of looking down into the toilet and seeing a mass of pinworms that have been passed puts us straight into denial. The largest parasite ever taken from a human that was weighed was over twenty pounds.

While some parasites are thought to cause little or no harm to their host, many cause great harm. For example, the protozoans that cause malaria are parasites that invade and destroy red blood cells and consequently take the lives of 3 million people worldwide every year. Some parasites are content to feed on the host's food supply while others go deeper and consume body tissues and cells, occasionally even burrowing through into our kidneys, muscles, corneas, and brain. A tapeworm can grow within us to a considerable size, and it's highly likely we will not be aware of it. Waste products from the parasites may be toxic and are released directly into the host's body. Infections from parasites wreak havoc in our immune systems, digestive tract, and can invade any of our other organ systems. Everything about parasites is gross and nasty.

A parasite is an organism that feeds and lives on another organism. A host is any animal that harbors a parasite. Parasites look for suitable habitat where they can thrive inside us, and most of the time they remain there uncontested. Some parasites not only live in us but also reproduce offspring that live in us, creating the potential for a serious parasitic infestation. There is no part of a human's body that is immune to parasites—not your organs, muscles, blood, brain, or lungs.

Some parasites are known to remain in the body for up to 10, 20, and even 30 years, depriving the body of nutrients and doing whatever damage they can do. And they are not known to respect the fact that someone is richer or higher class or young or old or man or woman or that they live in a certain part of the world. Anyone who is alive is a candidate for a parasite . . . and *Every Body* probably is infected.

Whenever I talk about parasites, the first reaction I get is: "This cannot be true inside of me!" I wish I could agree with them, but the statistics are not in their favor, and my professional experience points dramatically in the opposite direction. It is conservatively estimated that millions of people who live in the United States are suffering needlessly from chronic diseases that are primarily caused by parasites. A recent health report stated that 85 percent of Americans are infected with parasites. Dr. William Kelly, a famous cancer specialist, has stated that 92 percent of the people he treats test positive for parasites.

One would think that in a country where 50 to 55 million children are estimated to be hosts to some type of worms, regular screening for parasites would be a part of every medical checkup. But few health-care providers are taught to suspect, diagnose, or treat parasitic infections. If, for instance, you are suffering from diarrhea or fever and you go to your doctor, it is highly probable that he or she will treat the symptoms without even checking into a possible parasitic cause. And if a parasite is suspected, many of the test procedures for parasites are extremely inaccurate. If a parasite is found, an imprecise treatment may only cause the parasite to move to another spot, or it may kill that specific parasite while leaving others behind that were not detected. In the case to the tapeworm, if your treatment only expels the body and not the head, the whole worm will grow back—not what you want to hear.

Even alternative practitioners, naturopaths, and herbalists, who are generally more aware of the prevalence of parasitic infections, are not necessarily always able to identify their existence.

The truth is that however despicable it is to think that your own body may be a host to parasites, you are the greatest expert of what is going on in your body. The more you know about parasites and their symptoms, the better chance you have of remaining in or regaining vibrant health. When it comes to parasites, you may be the only one with the understanding of how to get rid of them and keep them out of your life.

SYMPTOMS, SOURCES, AND DISEASES ASSOCIATED WITH PARASITES

AS I SAID IN MY BOOK, *How to Feel Great All the Time*, wherever I go to give my seminars, whenever I'm on television, and whenever I open my e-mail, the constant complaint I get is this: "It's been a long time since I felt really good. I'm tired all the time. I'm exhausted and rundown. How can I start to feel good again?"

My career and travels put me in contact with a great number of people, and I am amazed at how few people can tell me they are living in great health. When people discover that I am a naturopathic doctor, they often launch into a wide range of chronic physical complaints. Some spell out personal symptoms of diverse emotional problems, some of which have resulted in anger and frustration or feelings of hopelessness and depression. Oftentimes they have consulted with their doctors but not found relief.

If you are experiencing a decline in health or a specific health problem, it usually has come on gradually and perhaps has been nearly undetectable. What is happening is that your body is sending you a signal that your body cells are in dis-ease for some reason. You have stepped out of homeostasis, "the state of being in health." Those body cells are not receiving the nutrients they need to sustain or propagate healthy cells, tissues, and organs. Dis-ease is associated generally with the absence or lack of some substance from our system, and/or a buildup of toxins in the bowels that needs to be eliminated. And it is very possible that the cause of what you are experiencing is directly due to parasites.

It can be as simple as this case from my own family. Many years ago, one of our children, who was three years old at the time, consistently complained that her "stomach hurts" at bedtime. Initially, my husband, Jim, and I thought it was the typical "I don't want to go to bed" syndrome. No big deal. But then I noticed she was grinding her teeth as well as drooling when she was sleeping. I was not a naturopath at the time, but I did my research, and every symptom pointed clearly to pinworms. I went to the health food store and found an herbal deworming formula that I was fairly certain would do the job. The pinworms were passed in her stool, and all the symptoms stopped as quickly. It wasn't pretty, but it was effective.

FOUR MAJOR FACTORS RELATED TO PARASITES

You need to be aware of these four major factors related to parasites:

1. Parasites are the source of many chronic health problems, and possibly yours.
2. Parasites and their symptoms range well beyond the

gastrointestinal tract, so don't limit your thinking. While most parasites that we host do come to reside in our 30 feet of gut, our lungs and blood and many other hiding places are also favorite parasitic homes as well as breeding grounds.

3. In similar fashion to the diagnosis of hypothyroidism and *Candida* (a parasitic yeastlike fungus), the symptoms caused by parasites will often mask themselves effectively beneath other ailments, and therefore often go undiagnosed. Many of the symptoms are subtle because they are experienced commonly by people without parasites. Thus, many doctors may correctly and consistently note their patients' fatigue, diarrhea, or irritability, but incorrectly attribute those symptoms automatically to wrong causes. For instance, a diagnosis of a peptic ulcer may rather be an infection from roundworms, or a case of giardiasis (an infection in the gut by water-borne microscopic protozoan *giardia*) may be misdiagnosed as chronic fatigue syndrome. It is also interesting to note that the diagnosis of liver cancer has been made by qualified physicians only to discover that what appeared to be cancer was actually a parasitical infestation or the eggs thereof.

4. Although parasites are masters of disguise and concealment, it's not surprising that just as there are road maps, navigational maps, and star maps, there are body maps. It's all a part of God's great plan for our lives, so when you visit your physician, he already has a map of sorts. The more frequent your visits, the better acquainted

you become with the doctor's process and routine. And similar to the shortcuts we take when we're in familiar territory, doctors have them too. They read the signs of coloration, eyes, ears, nose, throat, temperature, and a host of other indicators that lead them to a diagnosis or opinion. In many cases, parasites will erect road signs. This isn't their intention, far from it, but fortunately for us many of the signs or symptoms are hard to miss.

SYMPTOMS

The following list, while by no means exhaustive, reflects some of the common symptoms of parasites. See if you can relate to any of these:

- Allergies
- Anemia
- Apathy
- Asthma
- Bed-wetting
- Bloating
- Blood in stools
- Blurry or unclear vision
- Chronic fatigue
- Constipation
- Depression
- Diabetes
- Diarrhea
- Dizziness
- Eating more than usual but still being hungry
- Excess weight
- Fatty tumors, especially on feet
- Fevers
- Forgetfulness and mental slowness
- Gas
- Immune dysfunction
- Intestinal obstruction
- Irritability and nervousness
- Irritable bowel syndrome

- Itchy ears
- Itchy nose
- Itchy anus
- Lethargy
- Lips dry during the day and moist at night
- Nervousness
- Nutrient deficiencies, especially Vitamin B12 and folic acid
- Pain or aches in the back, joints, or muscles
- Problems with menstruation
- Sensitivity to touch
- Sexual dysfunction in men
- Sleep disorders
- Swollen glands
- Teeth clinching
- Teeth grinding
- Toxicity
- Unpleasant sensations in the stomach
- Various skin problems

You may be saying, "Some of these apply to *Every Body* at some time or another," and you're correct. As noted previously, parasites are not necessarily the cause of any of these symptoms, but they should not be dismissed. Perhaps what you're experiencing is just a case of poison ivy, but if the signs appear on a regular basis and the itching isn't somehow connected to a walk in the woods, you should pay attention to the signs. Remember, 80 to 90 percent of us have parasites and don't know it, so perhaps the best thing to do is go with the numbers, act as if you do, and make the decision to do something about it.

I recommend that you keep a journal of your symptoms, and particularly note symptoms that persist over time. It is vital to note any treatments you have received for a diagnosed problem that were not effective. This information could prove invaluable when you talk with your physician or naturopath.

I recently had a woman come to me who had been sick and had not worked for three years. She was a nurse, and none of the diagnoses she had received had affected the way she felt. I immediately recommended our product ParaCease, an herbal supplement that is formulated to help cleanse the body of unwanted Candida and parasites. She did the cleanse as I suggested, and soon thereafter she passed worms. After three long years, she instantly began to feet better.

If you remove the cause, the symptoms will cease, and vice versa. Unfortunately, parasitic causes are almost never even considered.

SOURCES

Because the range of parasites is so extensive, the range of sources is equally extensive. There is no way to avoid all contact with parasites, but there are common sources that you should be aware of.

Animals, particularly wild animals and farm animals, carry parasites. Small children tend to be especially exposed to parasitic contamination, including round-worms, through contact with animal feces in their yards or play areas. But pets also pose a formidable problem. Think of the multiplied millions of dogs and cats that are played with, slept with, and allowed to lick faces and snuggle, and then consider the potential parasitic roundworms and hookworms they carry, or the toxoplasmosis transmitted to humans by cats. While the routine deworming of pets is absolutely vital, that does not make your pet parasite-proof—reinfections can and do occur.

When a dog or cat is cleaning their coat, they are transferring parasites from their mouths to the hair by licking it. Those parasites may then be redeposited onto whatever they come into contact with. That may be your hand as a result of petting, or your bare feet from the carpet, or your arm from brushing the cushions of your couch or chair. Contaminations abound in our yards and within our homes. Cleaning carpets and furniture is a must if you have an inside pet.

And what about the bed? Mites are parasites and come from the Arachnid family. Sound familiar? Do you remember the movie *Arachnophobia*? It's about the fear of spiders. Well, these microscopic spiders are all over the place, including in your bed and pillows. If your favorite pillow is six years old or more, a full 10 percent of its weight could be from these mites, their carcasses and waste. Do you need to go to the pillow store today? As you can imagine, it is the wastes that pose most of the real danger. Mites love warm damp places and wait expectantly for their hosts to arrive each night so they can attach themselves to your body. Then they travel. How? It's really amazing. The dust in your house is made up of a number of things, but one of the primary components is dead skin, and guess what's on the dead skin—parasites. If you doubt that your body sheds that much, just rub your arm vigorously in a strong beam of light and watch the cloud of dead skin that appears. A family of four will produce a quart jar full of dead skin dust in a single month. This occurs in any other building where people work or congregate.

Fruits and vegetables. Whether it is contamination at the growing site or at the handling stage, most of us are aware that fruits and vegetables can carry a host of parasites. Billions upon billions of tons of food are imported every year, and some of those fruits and vegetables have been fertilized with human feces. For instance, contaminated raspberries imported from Guatemala caused almost 1,000 laboratory-confirmed cases of the *cyclospora* parasite to be reported to the Centers for Disease Control and Prevention (CDC) between May 1 and mid July 1996. But we're foolish to think similar contaminations are not happening in the fruits and vegetables grown and marketed locally. It happens all the time.

And while parasites are by no means limited to immigrant workers, the huge influx of immigrants who come from parasite-infected areas of the world and find jobs in the food service industry has increased the risk of parasite transmission exponentially. Add to that the fact that sanitation conditions in some food service facilities are abysmal, and it's no secret that we should avoid eating raw fruits and vegetables that have not been thoroughly cleansed. Soak your fruits and vegetables in a dilution of food grade peroxide available at your health food store or from Silver Creek Labs, which is listed in the back of the book.

Salad bars are prime sites for these parasites. There are chemicals that many restaurants apply to the salad bar to maintain freshness and prevent parasitic intruders, but if these chemicals are not applied appropriately, they may be harmful. And many times this responsibility is left up to a sixteen-year-old who could care less whether he or she follows the label directions.

Roaches are also primary carriers of parasites, and they're certainly not confined to restaurants. Roaches are in millions of households and schools and deposit parasites or their eggs everywhere they crawl.

Meats. Anyone who thinks that our supplies of beef, chicken, pork, and seafood are parasite-free is living on another planet. Despite the best efforts of the FDA to safeguard our food supplies, it is very possible that undercooked pork, fish, and beef carry tapeworms that will infect you if you partake of them. Raw meats and raw fish, however delicious and appealing, are a wide open door to the transmission of parasites. If you want to chance the raw fish in the sushi bar, realize that the risk is very real. The larvae from worms in fish such as the Pacific salmon or red snapper can enter your system and cause extensive damage. Be aware that wherever undercooking takes place within meat of every kind, the potential for transmission of parasites increases, and be especially aware that temperatures in microwaves often vary drastically within meat products.

Infected drinking water. I've already noted the outbreaks related to *cryptosporidium*, a water-borne parasite, which are not unusual, even within the United States. *Giardia lamblia* is another parasite that has found its way into

American water supplies and is not killed by chlorination. Wherever you have water systems that are exposed to infected human sewage or polluted watersheds, such as in rural America, you bring in the element of parasites.

Hot tubs, swimming pools, lakes, and rivers. The edges of warm water around a hot tub are frequent haunts of parasites. And the reality is that swimming pools, lakes, and rivers are easily contaminated. The next time you inadvertently gulp down a mouthful of water while swimming, realize that no matter how clear and pure it appears, it may be contaminated and primed to infect your system.

Day-care centers. If a child in a day-care facility has become infected with a parasite, it is an ideal environment for being passed along from one child to the next as well as to the day-care staff. For instance, giardiasis (a parasitic infection of the gut by the single-cell protozoan *giardia*) is spread through direct contact with infected feces, and changing diapers facilitates the transfer.

Overseas travel. The more you travel internationally, especially to Third World nations, and the more remote your destinations, the more you have the chance of encountering malaria or blood flukes or other serious parasitic infections. While the danger of parasites is constant and real in the United States, whole regions of the world are beset by parasites that we seldom face here. Our immune systems are not accustomed to pathogens from outside our living area, so start supplementing the immune system before a planned trip and consider doing an intestinal cleanse while you are traveling.

Basic hygiene. When it comes to parasites, one cannot stress enough the importance of washing your hands after touching and handling anything that might be contaminated—whether you've changed a diaper, gone to the bathroom, or handled food, especially raw meat or fish. And make certain that the toilet seat is clean before you sit on it; and if you can't do that, then squat over the toilet and don't touch it. Pinworm eggs from infected people may be on the seat, although you can't see them.

Sexual practices. Connected to basic hygiene, there is no question that today's careless attitudes of multiple sexual partners and practices have increased the transmission of parasites. The more that nonstandard contact is practiced, the proportional increase in infections that are spread to the hands, mouth, and body through fecal contamination. Anyone who believes that the use of a condom or a latex barrier in any type of sexual contact means complete protection is foolish.

And as if this list isn't already long enough, you'll discover that parasites love to hide in dish cloths, cutting boards, dishes, tabletops, vacuum cleaners, air ducts, kitty litter boxes, soil, sandboxes, mosquitoes, and ticks. There's no hiding from parasites.

DISEASES ASSOCIATED WITH PARASITES

■ Anemia
■ Chronic fatigue syndrome
■ Encephalitis
■ Epidemic typhus

- HIV
- Hyperinfection
- Irritable bowel syndrome
- Liver abscesses
- Lyme disease
- Low immunity
- Lymphatic filariae
- Malaria
- Pneumonia
- Scabies
- Sleeping sickness
- Toxoplasmosis
- Trichinella
- Ulcerative colitis
- Vitamin B-12 deficiency

ROUNDWORMS

JUST IN CASE YOU'RE COUNTING, THE ROUND-WORM, OR NEMATODE, probably always has been one of the most common parasites of man. Unfortunately for us, there are many different types of roundworms that can inhabit the human body—an estimated 10,000 species. While most of these worms are only a fraction of an inch long and fine as silk thread, some of them can reach lengths of 30 feet in whales. But for the purposes of this book, we'll limit ourselves to the major ones that impact humans the most and leave the whales to their own problems.

ROUNDWORMS (ASCARIS LUMBRICOIDES)

The large or giant intestinal roundworm is the most common intestinal parasite in the world. While an estimated 25 percent of the world's population is infected by it, in the United States the highest infestation is in the southern and Appalachian regions, where upwards of 64 percent of the population is infected. The female worm may be as thick as a pencil, and some reach from 6- to 12-inches long. Both sexes are creamy white in color. A mature female round-worm can produce an estimated 200,000 eggs daily . . . inside you.

Ascarid eggs are found in the soil contaminated by human feces or on fruits or vegetables grown in contaminated soil. Infection occurs when a person accidentally ingests (swallows) infective ascarid eggs. Children are easily infected by eating dirt or putting soiled hands into their mouths. Once in the human stomach, larvae (immature worms) hatch from the eggs. The larvae are carried through the lungs and then to the throat, where they are swallowed. Once swallowed, they reach the intestines and develop into adult worms, consuming a large amount of food and giving off their waste products. Adult female worms lay eggs that are then passed in feces. This entire cycle takes between 2 to 3 months.

"Roundworms create their own hydrogen peroxide (liquid oxygen) so that their offspring will be plentiful," says Hanna Kroeger, who is known as the "Grandmother of Health."

Most people have no symptoms from large or giant roundworms. If you are heavily infected, though, you may suffer abdominal pain. The worms may release a foreign protein that causes an allergic reaction. Sometimes, while the immature worms migrate through the lungs, you may cough, have difficulty breathing, and develop a lung infection. If you have a very heavy worm infection, your intestines may become blocked. Swelling of the lips, insomnia, anorexia, and weight loss can also be symptoms.

PINWORMS (ENTEROBIUS VERMICULARIS)

The pinworm is the most common roundworm in the United States. They are about the length of a staple, ivory or pearly white in color, live in the rectum of humans, and are very contagious. Day-care centers, schools, and other institutions where people are in close proximity often have cases of pinworm infection. It makes sense that school-age children, followed by preschoolers, have the highest rates of infection. In some groups nearly 50 percent of children are infected, and those infections are often compounded in more than one family member getting it as well. Adults are less likely to have pinworm infection, except mothers of infected children.

Adult pinworms inhabit the cecum (the large pouch forming the beginning of the large intestine) and other portions of the large and small intestines. The female pinworms crawl down the intestines and actually pass out of the anus to lay their eggs at night. A single female may deposit 5,000 to 15,000 eggs, which are infective immediately or within a few hours. The crawling of the worm on the skin of the perianal area often produces intense itching. The person scratches his bottom and contaminates his hands with the eggs, which is why they are often called seatworms. Thus the cycle continues.

The eggs also often attach themselves to the soiled linen in this region, contaminating bed linens and the person's pajamas or underwear. The eggs are readily transported through the air, and it is not uncommon to find them in every room of the house. Infection occurs by wearing clothes or sleeping in the bed of an infected person or through contact on the toilet seat or bathtub. The eggs stay viable for weeks, and reinfections become regular.

Pinworms are often found within the appendix and have been associated with acute and chronic inflammation. Heavy infestations of pinworms can cause insomnia, teeth grinding, nausea, hyperactivity, irritability, mental depression, and bed-wetting. Complications are much more common in women than in men. Pinworms have been found in the vagina, uterus, and fallopian tubes.

HOOKWORMS (NECATOR AMERICANUS, ANCYLOSTOMA DUODENALE)

One of the most common hookworm species, *Ancylostoma duodenale,* is found in southern Europe, northern Africa, northern Asia, and parts of South America. A second species, *Necator americanus,* was widespread in the southeastern United States early in the twentieth century. Hookworm infections occur mostly in tropical and subtropical climates and are estimated to infect about one-fifth of the world's population.

An adult hookworm is small, cylindrical, and grayish-white, with a head that is often curved in an opposite direction to the body. These are the only worms that have teeth. You can become infected by direct contact with contaminated soil when walking barefoot or accidentally by swallowing contaminated soil. The larvae enter the body through the skin, travel to the lungs, up the respiratory track until they are swallowed, and end up in the small intestines.

The hookworm grips on to the intestinal wall of humans with its teeth. It often penetrates the wall of the small intestine until it reaches a small blood vessel. Once it finds this vessel, it will inject an anti-coagulant into the blood to prevent the blood from clotting. In this way, the hookworm is insured of a small but steady supply of blood. The hookworm uses the hemoglobin in the blood to get oxygen to breathe.

Once established, the female adult worms produce from 15,000 to 20,000 eggs per day. These eggs are passed in the feces (stool). If the eggs contaminate soil and the conditions are right, they will hatch, molt, and develop into infective larvae again after 5 to 10 days. These worms can live up to 15 years in the body.

Itching and a rash at the site of where the skin touched the soil or sand and the larvae penetrated the skin is usually the first sign of infection. The severity of each hookworm infection is marked by the number of worms in the host's intestine and the nutritional state of the host. Hookworms usually cause mild diarrhea or cramps. Heavy infection can cause anemia, abdominal pain, diarrhea, listlessness, slowness, loss of appetite, and weight loss. Heavy, chronic infections can cause stunted growth and mental decline.

WHIPWORM (TRICHURIS TRICHIURA)

Whipworms, another type of roundworm that can be present in humans, are 30 to 50 millimeters long and shaped like a whip. The top two thirds is thin, and the bottom third is thicker, and they can be a couple inches long. Humans become infected through the ingestion of eggs in contaminated soil and water. Vegetables and fruits may also be contaminated with the eggs. The eggs develop in the small intestine from where they can later travel into the large intestine to mature. One female can lay 3,000 to 20,000 eggs a day. The life span of the adults is about one year.

A small number of whipworms may not cause any symptoms. Most of these worms live in the cecum, but a heavy infestation can lead them to be found throughout the entire colon. Heavy infections may include abdominal pain, nausea, insomnia, vomiting, gas, constipation, and headaches. Severe infections can involve bloody diarrhea, weight loss, anemia, and possible rectal prolapse, and even lead to death.

TRICHINELLA OR PORK ROUNDWORM (TRICHINELLA SPIRALIS)

This tiny spiral-shaped roundworm that causes trichinosis is found commonly in the United States and masquerades as many illnesses (from flu to generalized aches to specific pains to food poisoning). It is acquired by ingesting meat containing cysts (encysted larvae) of *Trichinella*, usually from pork that is not cooked thoroughly. One hundred thousand dormant, juvenile worms can be living within one ounce of infected meat. After exposure to the body's digestive juices, the larvae are released from the cysts and invade the small bowel mucosa where they develop into adult worms, then mate and release a huge number of young worms. These larvae migrate to the striated muscles where they encyst and may be found around the heart, brain, lungs, face, and throat. Encystment is completed in 4 to 5 weeks, and the encysted larvae may remain viable for several years. Ingestion of the encysted larvae perpetuates the cycle.

Light infections may be without symptoms. Intestinal invasion can be accompanied by a variety of gastrointestinal symptoms such as diarrhea, abdominal pain, and vomiting. Larval migration into muscle tissues (one week after infection) can cause severe muscle pain and periorbital and facial edema (swelling), inflammation of the eyes, fever, splinter hemorrhages, rashes, and blood eosinophilia. Occasional life-threatening manifestations include inflammation of the muscular substance of the heart, central nervous system involvement, and pneumonitis. Larval encystment in the muscles causes pain in the muscles and exhaustion, followed by a subsidence of symptoms.

STRONGYLOIDES OR THREADWORM (STRONGLYOIDES STERCORALIS)

This roundworm is similar to the hookworm, but is unique in that it can reproduce entirely in the human host or grow into a free-living worm in soil. The life cycle begins when larvae in contaminated soil penetrate the human skin and are transported to the lungs where they penetrate the alveolar spaces; they are carried through the bronchial tree to the pharynx, are swallowed, and then reach the small intestine. In the small intestine they molt twice and become adult female worms. The females live threaded in the cellular tissue that lines the small intestine and produce eggs, which can either be passed in the stool or can cause autoinfection. Reinfection can last for up to 30 years.

If a person has a strong functioning immune system, this parasite is often harmless. A weakened immune system allows this roundworm to go on to infect any organ or part of the body. The primary symptoms include abdominal pain, bloating, and diarrhea. Pulmonary symptoms (including Loeffler's syndrome) can occur during the pulmonary migration of the larvae. Dermatologic manifestations include itching, burning rashes in the buttocks and waist areas. Disseminated strongyloidiasis occurs in immuno-suppressed patients, can present with abdominal pain, distension, shock, pulmonary and neurologic complications and septicemia (toxins in the blood), and is potentially fatal. Blood eosinophilia is generally present during the acute and chronic stages, but may be absent with dissemination.

DOG AND CAT ROUNDWORM (TOXOCARA CANIS, TOXOCARA CATI)

Toxocariasis is an animal-to-human infection caused by the parasitic roundworms commonly found in the intestines of dogs (*Toxocara canis*) and cats (*T. cati*). Children are particularly vulnerable because of their playing habits and unsanitary habits around pets. In the United States, an estimated 10,000 cases of Toxocara infections occur yearly in humans.

Almost all puppies and kittens are infected and can produce large numbers of eggs that contaminate the environment through the animal's stool. The eggs soon develop into infective larvae and are ingested through dirty hands, handling pets, or eating fruits or vegetables that may have the eggs on them. The eggs will develop in the intestines where they mature and burrow into the circulatory or lymph system and finally reach the liver and lungs. This particular roundworm does not complete its life cycle in humans, but during its wandering through the body it can cause damage to the liver, lungs, heart, skeletal muscle, brain, and eyes.

Toxocara infections can cause OLM, an eye disease that can lead to blindness. Heavier or repeated Toxocara infections, while rare, can cause VLM, a disease that causes swelling of the body's organs or central nervous system. Symptoms of VLM, which are caused by the movement of the worms through the body, include fever, coughing, asthma, or pneumonia.

DOG HEARTWORM (DIROFILARIA IMMITIS)

This is a tiny roundworm that dwells in the blood and tissue in dogs and other mammals. It is transmitted through an infected mosquito, which passes the juvenile worms from host to host through its bite. The larvae seldom complete their life cycle in man, but the larvae live in the heart, blood vessels, and the lungs, causing a cough and chest pain. In heavy infections it can cause blockages of the blood vessels and damage body organs. If they do complete the life cycle in humans, they move to the lungs and become localized in a coin-like lesion that is easily mistaken for cancer. Those with low immune systems are more susceptible.

TAPEWORMS

TAPEWORMS ARE COMMON IN ALL PARTS OF THE WORLD AND ARE AMONG THE OLDEST PARASITES OF THE HUMAN RACE. These long, white, flat, ribbon-like parasites have neither mouths nor intestines and attach their heads (scolex) to the intestinal wall, where they absorb partially digested nutrients such as vitamin B12 and folic acid through their skin and then give off dangerous waste products. Below the head are individual segments (proglottids) that are generated one at a time to form the chain-like body. Each proglottid is a self-contained reproductive unit with both the male and female sex organs. As the worm matures, more and more segments are added.

BEEF TAPEWORM (TAENIA SAGINATA)

The beef tapeworm infestation occurs in people who eat raw or rare beef. The larva of the beef tapeworm often resides in the striated muscle of the cow where it develops into a bladder worm. The worm becomes protected by a calcified shell. When raw or undercooked beef is eaten by man, such as a rare steak, this bladder worm turns inside out and attaches to the mucous membrane of the intestinal wall. In about three months, it develops into an adult worm.

The beef tapeworm is the second largest tapeworm and can become 4 to 8 feet long and live as long as 25 years in its host. If there is any good news in this, it is the fact that usually only one tapeworm infects the system at one time.

Many people only realize they are infected when they discover sections of proglottids or whole pieces of the worm in their stool. In some people, the beef tapeworm can cause abdominal pains, weakness, loss of weight, nausea, dizziness, and other symptoms. If the head of this tapeworm digs too far into the intestinal wall, these injuries can be infected with bacteria and lead to ulceration of the intestinal wall. If this parasite ends up in the nervous system during the cyst phase, it can do neurologic damage that includes seizures and permanent disability (neurocysticercosis).

By the way, the ordinary freezing of raw beef does not kill the tapeworm larvae unless it is frozen for a prolonged period. Thoroughly cooked beef is the only safe way to go.

PORK TAPEWORM (TAENIA SOLIUM)

Pork tapeworms are similar to beef tapeworms but are shorter. They infect people through the eating of infested undercooked pork, such as ham or sausage. In the pork tapeworm, there are hooks in the head and suckers on the body which attach to the intestinal wall. Metabolic wastes from the tapeworm are absorbed by the host, producing toxic manifestations, and intestinal obstruction sometimes results from the balling-up of the worm.

This parasite can cause two types of infection in humans, one caused by the adult (an intestinal tapeworm infection) and one by the larval stage, which can affect any organ (cysticercosis). The infection by the adult stage is strictly a human intestinal infection, transmitted by ingestion of the encysted larval stage (*cysticerci*) of the worm from pork meat which then matures into the adult tapeworm. Infections caused by the larval stage itself can occur in either pigs or humans and are transmitted by eggs in human feces. Humans infected with the tapeworm shed the tapeworm eggs in their feces, and these can be ingested by either pigs or humans and develop into the larval stage. The disease cysticercosis can affect any organ, such as the heart, eyes, liver, spine, brain, and muscles. In pigs, the larvae encyst in the muscles and do not become mature worms; thus, eggs are not passed in pig feces. Cysticercosis is especially serious. In endemic areas it is a major cause of neurologic disease. Seizures and brain deterioration are possible. Infection in the United States is rare.

FISH TAPEWORM (DIPHYLLOBOTHRIUM LATUM)

The fish tapeworm is the largest of the human tapeworms. While it often grows to lengths of 3 to 7 feet, a fully developed worm may reach the length of 30 feet and have 3,000 to 4,000 segments in one worm. The main body of the worm—the proglottids—are virtually filled with male and female reproductive organs. This worm produces an incredible number of eggs, often more than 1,000,000 a day and billions during its lifetime!

Humans acquire the fish tapeworm by eating raw or

uncooked freshwater fish or certain migratory species of fish, such as Alaskan salmon, perch, pike, pickerel, and American turbot, where the adolescent tapeworm is embedded in the muscles. The adult fish tapeworm may live in man for 20 years or more and is most prevalent among populations that consume large amounts of freshwater fish. The fish tapeworms usually produce no visible symptoms. It can consume 80 to 100 percent of the host's vitamin B12. Pernicious anemia or a severe vitamin B12 deficiency is the most debilitating effect. Often the worm becomes so large that it should come as no surprise that it causes a colon blockage.

DWARF TAPEWORM (HYMENOLEPSIS NANA)

The dwarf tapeworm is found throughout the world, especially in tropical and subtropical areas, and wherever poor sanitary conditions are present. It is the most common tapeworm in the southern United States. Infection is most common in children, with contaminated soil passed from hand to mouth being the most frequent mode of transmission. Eggs are ingested from contaminated soil and develop into the cysticercoid stage. The cysticercoids attach to the mucosa of the small intestine and mature into adult worms. The adult worms lay eggs that may undergo maturation in the small bowel or pass through the host feces. It is only 1-1/2 inches long.

Most infections from the dwarf tapeworm are asymptomatic. When symptoms occur, they are usually limited to vague abdominal discomfort. Infections with a heavy worm load may lead to nausea, vomiting, weight loss, diarrhea, and more severe abdominal pain.

DOG TAPEWORM (DIPLYLIDIUM CANINUM AND ECHINOCOCCUS GRANULOSUS)

There is also a type of dog and cat tapeworm that can be passed to humans. The dog louse, the dog flea, and the cat flea serve as intermediate host, whereas humans are the final host after ingesting the louse or flea that contains the infective larvae. You can get the eggs of this worm on your fingers from the dog's hair or when the dog licks your face or hands.

In its host, the parasite attaches itself to the walls of the intestine. Its pregnant segments migrate through the anus or are passed through the feces to the outside world. The segments disintegrate and liberate their eggs to be swallowed by larval fleas. The parasite matures to larval stage with the flea, where it remains until a dog or cat ingests it, at which time it develops into the adult form.

These parasites infect humans and several other species, causing restlessness, abdominal pains, and painful bowel movements. The first indication of the infection may occur when finding pumpkin-seed-like particles in the stool. These particles are actually the egg-bearing segments or proglottids of the tapeworm.

FLUKES

FLUKES, ALSO KNOWN AS TREMATODA, ARE LEAF-SHAPED FLATWORMS with a bilaterally symmetrical body. These worms have suckers in the mouth that attach to blood vessels near the intestine and are parasitic during most of their life cycle no matter what form they assume. Flatworms lack a body cavity, a fluid filled region between the epidermis and the digestive tract. Flatworms also lack a complete digestive tract, but instead only have one opening for substances to both enter and leave the body. The smaller female fluke fits into a groove on the male, and they are often found attached, a position in which they can copulate freely. The eggs pass out in the host's feces, and the larvae can infect another organism and asexually divide to reproduce. Often, a fluke life cycle will involve living in more than one host.

Many species of flukes can infect humans, but they are typically grouped together in four types: blood, intestinal, liver, and lung flukes. They are the second most common form of parasite found in humans worldwide.

BLOOD FLUKE (SCHISTOSOMA)

Schistosomiasis, also known as bilharzia, is a disease caused by blood flukes. Infection with *Schistosoma mansoni*, *S. haematobium*, and *S. japonicum* causes illness in humans.

Although schistosomiasis is not found in the United States, 200 million people are infected worldwide.

Fresh water becomes contaminated by *Schistosoma* eggs when infected people urinate or defecate in the water. The eggs hatch, and if certain types of snails are present in the water, the parasites grow and develop inside the snails. The parasite leaves the snail and enters the water where it can survive for about 48 hours. *Schistosoma* parasites can penetrate the skin of persons who are wading, swimming, bathing, or washing in contaminated water. Within several weeks, worms grow inside the blood vessels of the body and produce eggs. Some of these eggs travel to the bladder or intestines and are passed into the urine or stool.

Within days after becoming infected, the person may develop a rash or itchy skin. Fever, chills, cough, and muscle aches can begin within 1 to 2 months of infection. Most people have no symptoms at this early phase of infection. Eggs travel to the liver or pass into the intestine or bladder. Rarely, eggs are found in the brain or spinal cord and can cause seizures, paralysis, or spinal cord inflammation. For people who are repeatedly infected for many years, the parasite can damage the liver, intestines, lungs, and bladder.

INSTESTINAL FLUKE (FASCIOLOPSIS BUSKI)

These flukes occur mainly in Southeast Asia and the Indian subcontinent, especially in areas where humans raise pigs and consume freshwater plants. Typically, the fluke is transmitted when people bite into the unpeeled outer skin of plants (water chestnuts, bamboo shoots, and lotus plant roots) that harbor the cyst form of this parasite. The adult fluke lives in the small intestine where it can cause ulcerations. Most infections are light and asymptomatic. In heavier infections, symptoms include diarrhea, nausea, vomiting, abdominal pain, fever, and intestinal obstruction.

Dr. Hulda Clark has claimed that the intestinal fluke causes "all diseases"—cancer and HIV and AIDS—and several web sites use these claims in their advertisements to sell various cures for these diseases. There are no peer-reviewed, published, scientific studies demonstrating that *Fasciolopsis buski* causes any of these diseases in humans.

LIVER FLUKE (CLONORCHIS SINENSIS)

The liver fluke is very common in Asia, including Korea, China, Taiwan, and Vietnam. Clonorchiasis has been reported in non-endemic areas, including the United States. In such cases, the infection is usually found in Asian immigrants or following ingestion of imported, under-cooked, or pickled freshwater fish containing encysted parasites. They can live for a decade, dining off our livers. Most pathologic manifestations result from inflammation and intermittent obstruction of the bile-carrying ducts. In the acute phase, abdominal pain, nausea, diarrhea, and eosinophilia can occur. In long-standing infections, cholangitis, cholelithiasis, pancreatitis, and cholangiocarcinoma can develop, which may be fatal.

LUNG FLUKE (PARAGONIMUS WESTERMANI)

More than 30 species of flukes of the genus *Paragonimus* have been reported which infect animals and humans.

Among the more than 10 species reported to infect humans, the most common is *P. westermani*, the oriental lung fluke. While *P. westermani* occurs in the Far East, other species of *Paragonimus* are encountered in Asia, the Americas, and Africa. The lung fluke enters the human body via insufficiently cooked or raw crabs and crayfish that are infected.

The lung fluke can perforate and weaken the lungs and even cause oxygen starvation of the entire bloodstream. The acute phase (invasion and migration) may be marked by diarrhea, abdominal pain, fever, cough, urticaria, hepato-splenomegaly, pulmonary abnormalities, and eosinophilia. During the chronic phase, pulmonary manifestations include cough, expectoration of discolored sputum, hemoptysis, and chest radiographic abnormalities. Extrapulmonary locations of the adult worms result in more severe mani-festations, especially when the brain is involved.

PROTOZOANS

THIS IS A LARGE CLASSIFICATION OF PARASITES WHICH ARE ESSENTIALLY FOUND WORLDWIDE in most soils, fresh water, and oceans—everywhere in our environment. Protozoans are groups of organisms that consist of a single cell and are usually microscopic. While most are solitary individuals, various colonial forms exist. Through their intensely rapid reproductive ability, certain protozoans can take over the intestinal tract of their host and from there go on to other organs and tissues. Most of them are transmitted through fecal contaminated food and impure water.

The protozoans are a diverse group. The smallest known protozoans are tiny blood parasites less than 2 microns long; the largest may be 16 mm long and visible to the naked eye. Protozoan shapes vary, but all share such eukaryotic features as lipid-protein membranes and membrane-enclosed vacuoles and organelles. Some protozoans produce cysts—closed sacs in which they may be safely transported through food and water from one person to another. They show wide variation in modes of movement (such as microscopic whiplike flagellae), nutrition, and reproduction and are categorized based on those modes.

Within this chapter I will only be dealing with an

extremely limited number of protozoans—the list is almost endless. Previously in the book I have mentioned, for instance, the *cyclospora* parasite and the *cryptosporidium* parasite, both protozoans that have been the source of several outbreaks of infection in the United States over the past years. Fungi, viruses, and bacteria will not be covered here.

AMOEBAS

These protozoans move by extending blunt lobelike projections of the cytoplasm called pseudopods.

One example of a pathogenic (disease-causing) protozoan is *Entamoeba histolytica*, which causes amoebic dysentery and is among the top life-threatening parasitic diseases. They can spread from person to person through food or water, or they can spread indirectly through fecal-oral contact and by direct contact with contaminated hands or objects, and by sexual contact. Approximately 450 million people are infected every year, which can lead to death.

When cysts are ingested, they are first carried to the small intestine, where it grows and multiplies and feeds on bacteria, tissue, and blood cells. It is possible for it to penetrate the wall of the intestine and invade the liver, lungs, brain, and heart.

On average, about one in 10 people who are infected with *E. histolytica* becomes sick from the infection. The other 90 percent may never realize how close they were to life-threatening problems. The symptoms often are quite mild and can include loose stools, stomach pain, and stomach cramping. Amoebic dysentery is a severe form of amebiasis associated with stomach pain, bloody stools, and fever. Rarely, *E. histolytica* invades the liver and forms an abscess. Even less often, it spreads to other parts of the body, such as the lungs or brain.

FLAGELLATES

Flagellates have a flagellum, a whip-like structure that allows them to be pulled through the medium. In some cases, the flagellum is attached to an undulating membrane. A few diseases caused by flagellates are giardiasis (beaver fever, caused by *giardia lamblia*), trichomonas infection (caused by *Trichomonas vaginalis*), and Chagas' disease is caused by the flagellate, *Trypanosoma cruzi,* and closely resembles the African sleeping sickness (*Trypanosoma brucei*).

Giardia is the name of a microscopic parasite that can live in the human bowel and is one of the most infectious parasitic invaders. Giardiasis is easy to catch if you drink untreated spring water or stream water, and the result is usually intestinal distress. Many animals carry *giardia* in their feces, particularly beaver, and may introduce this parasite into rivers, streams, and springs in rural areas. Infected stream water may look clean and safe when it really isn't. City water may also be infected if sewer lines flood or leak. If you travel overseas, you may get giardiasis by drinking water that hasn't been boiled or treated.

Once a cyst is ingested, the *giardia* changes to its next stage and multiples. It can coat the lining of the intestine and prevent digestion and assimilation of foods as well as absorb nutrients from the intestinal tract. It thrives on excess proteins and vitamins, and seems to afflict men worse than women. Some symptoms of giardiasis are diarrhea, belching, gas, greasy stools, and abdominal cramping. Although these problems are very unpleasant, the illness isn't usually dangerous. Some people who get giardiasis don't become ill, but they may spread the parasite to other people. Giardiasis may be spread in day-care centers if workers aren't careful to wash their hands each time after changing diapers. The CDC reports that approximately 2 million Americans are infected with *giardia* annually.

Trichomonas infection is caused by *Trichomonas vaginalis,* a microscopic parasite found worldwide that lives in the vagina and urinary tract of females and the prostate, seminal vesicles, and urinary tract of males. Trichomoniasis is one of the most common sexually transmitted diseases, mainly affecting 16- to 35-year-old women, especially women who have had multiple sexual partners. In the United States, it is estimated that 2 million women become infected each year. Signs and symptoms of infection range from having no symptoms (asymptomatic) to very symptomatic. Typical symptoms include foul smelling or frothy green discharge from the vagina, vaginal itching, or redness. Other symptoms can include painful sexual intercourse, lower abdominal discomfort, and the urge to urinate. Most men with this infection do not have symptoms. When symptoms are present, they most commonly are discharge from the urethra, the urge to urinate, and a burning sensation with urination.

Trypanosoma cruzi causes trypanosomiasis, the

American sleeping sickness known as Chagas' disease. The parasite is found throughout much of central and northern South America, Central America, Mexico, and southwestern United States. Transmission occurs through the bite of a large winged insect carrier. Most infections do not produce any symptoms. Chronic infections result in various neurological disorders, including dementia, megacolon, and megaesophagus, and damage to the heart muscle. Left untreated, Chagas' disease is often fatal.

CILIATES

The ciliates possess cilia, which are tiny hairlike structures that beat in a rhythmic fashion and are found covering the surface of the cell. *Balantidium coli*, which causes balantidiasis, is the only ciliate known to cause a human disease. The cysts of this parasite are transmitted by food and water contaminated with pig and occasionally monkey feces. Person-to-person transmission usually involves food handlers. It usually resides in the large intestine where it can invade and destroy the wall lining. Most cases are asymptomatic. Clinical manifestations, when present, include persistent diarrhea, occasionally dysentery, abdominal pain, and weight loss. Symptoms can be severe in debilitated persons.

SPOROZOANS

The sporozoans do not have structures for movement. The most common sporozoan are the various species of *Plasmodium* that cause malaria, all transmitted by the bite of an infected anopheles mosquito. Once established, the parasites invade the red blood cells and destroy them. The symptoms of uncomplicated malaria can be rather non-specific and the diagnosis can be missed if health providers are not alert to the possibility of this disease. Since untreated malaria can progress to severe forms that may be rapidly (24 hours) fatal, malaria should always be considered in patients who have a history of exposure.

The most frequent symptoms include fever and chills, which can be accompanied by headache, myalgias, arthralgias, weakness, vomiting, and diarrhea. Other clinical features include splenomegaly, anemia, thrombocytopenia, hypoglycemia, pulmonary or renal dysfunction, and neurologic changes. The clinical presentation can vary substantially depending on the infecting species, the level of parasitemia, and the immune status of the patient. Infections can progress to severe, potentially fatal forms with central nervous system involvement (cerebral malaria), acute renal failure, severe anemia, or adult respiratory distress syndrome. Nearly 3 million people worldwide still die of malaria yearly.

While it's not possible to cover the full gamut of Protozoans, there is one more that I need to mention for the sake of everyone who has a cat for a pet. Toxoplasmosis is an infection caused by a single-celled parasite called *Toxoplasma gondii* and is acquired from cats. It can also be ingested through eating or contact with infected raw or partly cooked meat, and through drinking water contaminated by it. More than 60 million people in the United

States probably carry this parasite, but very few have symptoms because the immune system usually keeps the parasite from causing illness. However, pregnant women and those with compromised immune systems should be cautious of this infection. This parasite can reproduce dramatically and cause serious disease.

You may feel like you have the flu, swollen lymph glands, or muscle aches and pains that last for a month or more. Chronic-phase symptoms include hepatitis and, in some cases, blindness. Because of the lymph involvement, toxoplasmosis can be misdiagnosed as Hodgkin's disease. Infants who are infected while in the womb have no symptoms at birth but may develop symptoms later in life. Only a small percentage of infected newborns have serious eye or brain damage at birth.

CANDIDA

AMONG THE MANY PARASITIC BACTERIA THAT CAN AFFECT OUR LIVES, the tiny yeastlike fungus *Candida albicans* is the one that I deal with the most. Since the time of Hippocrates (400 B.C.), yeast infections have been recognized as a problem. For hundreds of years it has been known that *Candida*, which lives naturally in all healthy bodies, can cause vaginal problems and skin and mouth rashes. But never before have they plagued the human race so intensely as they do today. Seven out of ten women get at least one attack of *Candida* overgrowth or thrush in their lives. It is also common for babies to develop this in their diaper area or in their mouths.

Candida is a parasitic yeastlike fungus that exists naturally in the body and usually causes no bad effects. It mainly inhabits the digestive tract but can spread to other parts of the body such as the esophagus, mouth, throat, genital area, and even the lungs in severe cases. In a normal healthy body, these harmless parasites coexist in small colonies along with the other bacteria found in our digestive system. These "colonies" of the *Candida* are anaerobic organisms (existing in the absence of oxygen), and when they occur in large numbers, they can release their toxic waste directly into the bloodstream, which can cause any of the symptoms noted below. It is estimated that over 90 percent of the U.S. population has some degree of *Candida* overgrowth in their bodies.

The immune system and the "friendly" bacteria in our intestines (*Bifidobacteria bifidum* and *Lactobacillus acidophilus*) keep *Candida* overgrowth under control most of the time in a healthy body. These bacteria and others make up the normal bacterial population of our gastrointestinal tract and are often referred to as "GI microflora." They exist in a symbiotic relationship with us and are essential for maintaining healthy intestines and resisting infections. However, when an imbalance occurs in the natural bacterial environment, which can be caused by a variety of reasons, then the *Candida* begin to grow at a rapid rate and spread and infect the body tissues.

For instance, the extended use of antibiotics prescribed for all kinds of infections is one of the reasons for the prevalence that we now see with the *Candida*. Antibiotics destroy not only the disease-causing bacteria but also the "friendly" bacteria that help to control the *Candida* bacteria. As a result, an imbalance occurs in the pH levels of our intestines, which in turn stimulates the growth of the *Candida*. Antibiotics are also found in many foods as residue, resulting from their use in food animals.

Other contributing factors are oral contraceptives and cortisone-type steroids. These types of drugs cause a hormone imbalance and weaken the body, which also favors the growth of *Candida*. The average American diet is also a cause for *Candida*. A lot of the food we consume is over-processed, high in refined sugar and carbohydrates, colored, and low in fiber. It is no wonder that we have a problem with yeast infections when you consider all the fast-food we eat in our fast-paced society. Our lifestyles have drastically affected our eating habits. According to a *Journal of American Medical Association* article in 1977, this kind of diet results in fewer "friendly" bacteria in our gastrointestinal tract. Those conditions then favor the onset of Candidiasis.

It can be one of these causes or a combination of all of them to different degrees that can throw our bodies out of balance. The human body is "fearfully and wonderfully made," but it has its limits also. When we cross those limits, and a serious flare-up of Candidiasis occurs, then we may experience a variety of alarming symptoms.

Yeast infections can occur in anybody at any age, but they are more prevalent in women. When our body systems become imbalanced, then a yeast overgrowth can occur. It is possible for someone to have a problem for a while before they manifest symptoms.

A host of symptoms that can be caused by *Candida* overgrowths:

- abdominal pain
- acne
- adrenal problems
- arthritis
- athlete's foot
- bad breath

- bloating
- brain fog
- burning tongue
- canker sores
- chronic fatigue
- cold hands or feet

- clogged sinuses
- colitis
- congestion
- constipation
- depression
- diarrhea
- even diabetes
- gas
- headaches
- head pain
- hyperactivity
- hypothyroidism
- immune weakness
- impotence
- Jock itch
- kidney and bladder infections
- memory loss
- mood swings
- muscle and joint pain
- mucous in stools or vaginal area
- nagging cough
- nail fungus
- night sweats
- numbness in the face or extremities
- persistent heartburn
- PMS
- poor digestion
- poor elimination
- prostatitis
- rectal itching
- severe itching
- skin rashes
- sugar and carbohydrate cravings
- sore throat
- tingling sensations
- vaginitis
- white spots on the tongue and in the mouth

If you suffer from any of these symptoms, there is a chance that it may be yeast-related. From my years of treating *Candida*, I can assure you that it will disguise itself in everything from athlete's foot to low blood sugar to obesity. *Disguise* is the operative word for *Candida*.

Symptoms often worsen in damp and/or moldy places,

and after consumption of foods containing sugar and/or yeast, as well as after a round of antibiotics. Because this disorder is oftentimes misdiagnosed, many individual symptoms are treated, but the sufferer from *Candida* often never gets to the root of the problem.

Candida can exist in two forms: yeast and fungal. Serious health problems can develop when it changes its anatomy to a fungal form. In that state, the organisms produce rhizoids (very long rootlike structures) that penetrate the mucous lining of the intestines. These rhizoids leave tiny holes that break down the natural barrier between the intestines and the circulatory system and allow toxins, bacteria, yeast, and even small undigested food particles direct access to the bloodstream. Once these toxins enter the bloodstream, they can travel throughout the entire body and produce a number of adverse symptoms that further weaken the immune system.

I encourage you, if you feel there is any chance that you may have a yeast problem, to read chapter 5 of my book, *How to Feel Great All the Time*, or my booklet *How to Stop Candida and Other Yeast Conditions in Their Tracks*. Both contain a Self-Analysis Test to help you discover to what degree you may be affected. Decide if you should do a *Candida* cleanse which is further described in both the book and the booklet. I offer a new product in tablet form called *Candida Cleanse* that can eliminate the overgrowth as well as help to normalize bowel functions.

ELIMINATING PARASITES

THE PRIMARY REASON YOU ARE READING THIS BOOK RIGHT NOW is because you probably don't want unknown and harmful parasites to remain living in your body. It is not enough to deal with the symptoms of infection. The parasites must be eradicated or they will continue to do their damage. Something you've read, heard someone say, or perhaps seen on TV has caused you to take action. And that action involves finding a way to eliminate the creepy-crawlies, get them out of your body, and far, far away. Part of this removal process is "elimination"— purging them from your entire body.

I have made it clear that parasites can live almost everywhere in the human body. They can live and reproduce in your brain, eyes, lungs, under the skin, in the feet, and intestines. As a matter of fact, you are probably in some stage of passing parasites right now and don't even recognize it. They do have a life cycle, some longer than others, but eventually they die and pass through the host body.

But during their life cycle they can do extensive damage through what they eat, digest, and eliminate. Their elimination is toxic, and that is a big part of the danger. Perhaps more sinister is a parasite's reproductive cycle. Some can lay almost one million eggs a month, and these babies do the same things as their parents and take up where their parents left off when they die. So it can be a never-ending cycle, even though you, the host, may never even see them.

We had a man come to our office, and while he was with us a living parasite actually passed out of his body through the corner of his eye. Other people will feel little pellets the size of a grain of salt or rice in their scalp and think it's just atmospheric dust or dandruff. Parasites may suddenly appear or be ignored, but they are nevertheless real.

So how do we get rid of parasites?

CLEANSING MUST BEGIN IN THE INTESTINES

The Royal Academy of Physicians of Great Britain states that "90 percent of all disease and discomfort is directly or indirectly related to an unclean colon (due to impacted fecal matter)." If we wish to eliminate the problems brought on by parasites, it's obvious that it begins with cleansing our intestines.

The account of the elimination of waste from our system began with the first man. Our makeup may have changed slightly as the world has become more toxic, but the principles of eating, digesting, and eliminating remain the same. Unfortunately, our diets have also changed. We no longer live on nuts, berries, fruits, vegetables, and other products from the garden.

We think we've come a long way, now that we radiate foods, add chemicals, and actually invent mouth-watering edibles right out of a vat. But not only are these things bad for us, it's apparent how bad they are when the parasites refuse to eat the stuff that comes out of the vats. We partake and end up with weakened and compromised immune systems that are not strong enough to fight off the parasitic invaders.

As civilization progressed, foods did change and the consumption of other foods that weren't compatible contributed to digestive and disease problems. If you recall in the Old Testament, Solomon warned his readers to "be not desirous of [a ruler's] dainties: for they are deceitful meat" (Proverbs 23:3, KJV). Many years later, Daniel, Hanaiah, Mishael, and Azariah refused to eat King Nebuchadnezzar of Babylon's "royal food and wine" because it was defiling (Daniel 1:8). They were committed to the ancient Levitical Diet, which I still feel is the best diet for your health. I'll have much more to say about that later, but there is no substitute for a proper diet to help cleanse the intestines and keep them clean.

These wrong foods and incompatible choices created a need for help. So we find the earliest physicians or their counterparts administering aid in the form of what is now known as an enema. Greeks, Romans, and Egyptians all record using this remedy for a clogged colon. As a matter of documentation, the phenomena only continued to grow throughout the ages, and as late as the seventeenth century we find King Louis the XIII receiving at least 200 such treatments in a single year.

This ancient technique has largely been abandoned to the use of drugs or chemical laxatives used by approximately 70 million Americans at a cost of over $400,000,000 dollars a year and necessitates an estimated 100,000 surgeries a year. There is a better way, and all of this involves the subject of parasites.

Cleansing your bowels is a key part in this process of the elimination of parasites. The intestines provide parasites with an abundance of food and very little interference to their activities. As parasites die off, they travel through your body in the same way most other waste and debris do, finally being dumped out through the bowels. Most of the parasites that are actually seen and collected by their former hosts are passed during a bowel movement. There are people who have no interest in discovering what comes out. They'll go through an entire parasite cleanse and never take a look. One such woman said, "I just go and run." And that's fine, but the point is, go!

Regular elimination during a parasite cleanse is vital. A cleanse that does not include ingredients that will help establish a regular pattern of three or more bowel movements a day should be reconsidered. If you are one of those people who wonders how many times a day your bowels should move, you need only think of a newborn baby. With each feeding, the baby's bowels will generally move. Adults, too, should be that regular. But that isn't usually the case.

CONSTIPATION INVITES PARASITES

Seventy percent of Americans are overweight, and along with the excess weight comes constipation. But you may be one of the few who is saying, "I'm not overweight, and I only defecate once a day, or maybe once every two days, maybe even once a week!" Well, I consult with a number of people just like you, and the point isn't how much you weigh, it's how healthy your bowels are, and how often they move.

Are you regular every day? This is very important. Your colon is a sewage system, and similar to the one in your house, it's dangerous and unhealthy if it gets backed up.

This actually happened to one of my neighbors. One night while everything else was uneventful, a slow developing clog in the sewage system reached its limit and a pipe broke from the pressure. Raw sewage spilled out everywhere, covering an entire floor of the home. The firemen came and did what they could, then the insurance adjuster showed up and ordered a professional restoration company to come in and clean up the horrible mess. But something even more serious was uncovered during the clean up. The pros found "Black Mold" hidden in the walls, the ceiling, and every room in the house.

Black mold poses many serious health problems, so the insurance company moved our friends out and went to work, attempting to eliminate the mold. It took six agonizing months, during which our friends lived in an apartment on the other side of town. Completely inconvenienced and feeling a bit displaced, they drove farther to school, work, bank, church, and everywhere else they had been accustomed to going during the previous 15 years of ownership. But when they came home, the diseased house was restored to health. Praise God for alerting these wonderful people to the true enemy concealed within their home. There's no telling what effect this could have had on the family's long term health. Similar to insidious hidden parasites in a human, this house had a serious problem that was waiting to be discovered.

This story has profound relevance to your situation. You may be living in a body, which God calls your temple, that's full of hidden dangers. If your plumbing is clogged, you may be in for a big surprise just as our neighbors were. But be of good cheer, from what you're learning in this book, you'll know to call in the professionals before that day of disaster occurs. "Who ya gonna call?"

So while being overweight significantly contributes to constipation, no matter what size you are, the important question is whether your bowels move as frequently as I suggested they should. If not, you must take action involving the elimination process. It is imperative that if you are going to go through the parasite cleanse that it include a product that will gently guide you back into a regular cycle of waste elimination. We tell everyone who uses our ParaCease cleanse that we hope they will have three movements a day, on their own, after 90 days on the program.

THE PROBLEM RESTATED

There is a well-publicized autopsy of a famous pop singing star who was reported to have an amazing amount of toxic waste backup in his colon at the time of his death. How many pounds would qualify for your definition of amazing? 10, 20, 30 pounds? A large newborn baby, for instance, won't weigh more than 10 to 12 pounds, and yet the mother-to-be is usually huge prior to birth, so that's a lot, right? Well, a large newborn is about a quarter of the weight found in this plump celebrity. While the reports vary upward, it was estimated that 40 or more pounds of fecal waste were packed in his colon! That is amazing.

Dr. Bernard Jensen said, "The average person over 40 has between 5 and 25 pounds of build up in their colon. Parasites of all sizes thrive in this indisposed residue of fecal matter, slowly but surely toxifying the whole body." *Toxicity* is a harmful effect (like that of a poison) that some substances have on the body. The effect can be minor or major and may only be found with special tests (a person may not know it is even happening). The harmful effect can last a very short time, a few weeks to months, or sometimes be permanent.

The average person is walking around with 7 to 10 pounds of waste, and that's not good either. Fecal encrustations are built up slowly and interfere with the absorption of nutrients. We must take control and clean the pipes out—all of them. Not just the main drain but everything. Your bowels are first, but we want to go further, all the way down to the cellular level. How else do you think I propose we get unwanted rubbish out of our brain, eyes, ears, joints, heart, lungs, intestines, and so on? The parasite cleanse does play a major part and is the commander and chief in this process, but it can't do it all by itself. More help is required for maximum benefits, and most of our systems just aren't where they need to be if we want to live in fullness of health.

So where can we enlist the best defensive force in this war on parasites? First, the parasite cleansing product needs to be superior. It should include natural ingredients that assist your colon's natural movement. If not, it's going to be up to you to investigate and find a natural product that will accomplish this goal. I'm often asked if I'm advocating laxatives at this point, and the answer is no, at least

e typical sense of a chemical laxative. I don't just
e-time movement, and I certainly don't want anyone becoming addicted to laxatives. The product must be
one that re-trains the whole system to function on its own.
This won't happen overnight or with the products you see
advertised on television. It takes time and must be proven
effective for long-term results.

COLON ASSISTANTS—ENEMAS

Nowadays it seems as though most people aren't familiar with this topic, so I'll offer a description. An enema is a
process whereby the lower bowel, which is approximately
five feet long, accepts liquid into it whereby the bowel will
begin to contract and force elimination of the waste mate-
rial. There are a couple of ways this can be accomplished,
but as with so many things the old fashioned way seems
the best. That is an enema bag, a rubber bladder that holds
a couple of quarts of water and is attached to a hose and tip
that accompanies it when purchased. Sometimes a little
lubricant is helpful, and both may be obtained at your local
pharmacy or grocery.

My recommendation is to use the enema bag system
along with distilled water. Distilled water is the most pure
water available and is also readily on hand at the stores
mentioned above. And no matter if it's an enema or a
colonic, any equipment used must be thoroughly steril-
ized. Fecal matter can transmit disease and easily passes
along parasitic contaminates.

For a successful enema we suggest you include coffee

in the distilled water solution. I've heard some really weird stories when people tell me how they've accomplished this—or at least tried—but the recommended way is very simple. First, brew a pot of coffee. However you do that in your home is the way you would do it now. It doesn't matter whether it's by percolator, drip, or pressed, but use one teaspoon of coffee per cup and proceed as usual. *No instant or decaffeinated coffee is allowed!* After making the coffee, add two cups to your room temperature water that you've already placed into the enema bag. Hang the bag and follow the directions provided by the bag's manufacturer.

During this process it's good to massage your colon and liver. This will cause the coffee to work farther up into the colon, thus giving you a more effective bowel movement. The liver, which is the key detoxifying organ in your body, is also very important in this process. In the course of the coffee enema and massage, the liver will want to dump, releasing toxins and parasites that may have built up in it.

Be wise in your application and read the manufacturer's instructions closely. It is possible in the case of children to perforate the bowels and cause ruptures.

COLONICS OR COLON HYDROTHERAPY

Fundamentally, the process of colonics, otherwise known as colon hydrotherapy, is the same as an enema. Water is infused and expelled, but that's where the similarity ends. The administration is different, usually involving a colon therapist and specialized equipment, and the outcome is usually superior to an enema.

An enema involves taking in as much of the water contained in the enema bag as possible, holding it in for as long as possible, then releasing it and you're finished. Colonics, however, entail repetitive infusions that irrigate into the entire length of the upper and lower colon. Warm water is gently introduced through a special tube, and at the same time waste passes out through another tube. The whole experience is usually pleasant and lasts for 45 minutes to an hour. I recommend this process and suggest that you call my office for a Certified Colon Therapist in your area.

COLEMA BOARD

This devise is a manual colonic that a person can utilize by himself. It involves a board that's about three and a half feet long with an opening at the base, which is placed over the toilet and the other end is supported by a chair or the like. A five-gallon bucket is filled with lukewarm water and placed in a position above the board, then a tube is placed in the water bucket, run down into the back of the Colema board, and attached to a tip that is then inserted into the rectum. A clamp is attached to the tubing, which allows the user to control the flow of the water. Gravity moves the water in and can be very effective for home use.

Many people involved in a parasite cleanse will insert a colander in the bowl to easily examine what might pass through.

DIGESTIVE ENZYMES AND PROBIOTICS

During a cleanse you should take digestive enzymes to dissolve the protective shell that surrounds some parasitic cysts.

And whenever you have completed an intestinal cleanse, always follow it with a good probiotic, and do it daily. It creates a good terrain for aerobic bacteria (good bacteria) to live and thrive in and is a first line of defense against any intruders.

Taking probiotics allows people to achieve optimum health by supplying them with the nutrients they would ordinarily be receiving had they eaten food derived from nutrient-dense soil. Probiotics are beneficial bacteria, which live in pure, nutrient-rich soil and are responsible for providing plants (vegetables and fruits) with those nutrients they require. The probiotics are absorbed by plants and become their protectors against harmful invaders. In that way probiotics keep plants healthy and loaded with nutritional components as a source of food for humans. The same thing occurs for humans when we ingest the friendly organisms as nutritional supplements. These friendly organisms keep the human GI tract in a state of homeostasis by increasing intestinal absorption and keeping it free of parasites, yeasts, molds, other fungi, harmful bacteria, viruses, and additional pathogens such as spirochetes, rickettsiae, chlamydiae, protozoa, and helminths. Probiotics can turn really aggressive against pathological invaders and have an amazing ability to engulf and ingest viruses and bacteria. They also stimulate the formation of Lactoferrin (the iron-binding protein that exerts antimicrobial activity by withholding iron from any harmful microorganisms that the patient ingests).

Probiotics (the opposite of antibiotics) restore balance to an autointoxicated gastrointestinal tract in a specific manner.

Upon being swallowed, the probiotic will activate and bring about gut restoration by attaching themselves to the intestinal mucosa. On the gut wall they reproduce to form colonies along the course of "receptor sites" that had previously been established by harmful bacteria and other pathological microorganisms. These pathogens are crowded out or eaten up by the probiotics so that the symptoms of illness they had been producing tend to terminate eventually. The time factor for symptomatic healing is dependent upon the volume of pathogens lodged at the gut's receptor sites. No matter what the number of bad bacteria or other pathogens, probiotics implant themselves and bring about gut restoration.

Medical journalist Ann Louise Gittleman affirms that once colonized in the GI tract, these probiotics eventually balance the colonic pH to set the stage for restoring all the body systems. She states that the survival of some of the gut's most important resident microorganisms, such as *Lactobacillus acidophilus,* depends on the visiting probiotic byproduct. The probiotic content of each person's gastrointestinal tract is an integral part of his or her immune system.

FOODS TO HELP DEFEAT THE BUGS

- Consider the ParaCease program that's described in the Silver Creek Labs section in the back of the book. It comes with a dietary program.
- Use apple cider vinegar with each meal.
- Almond oil
- Increase protein intake
- Cranberries and cranberry juice

- Garlic
- Pomegranates
- Pumpkin seeds
- 8 to 10 glasses of good water per day. Clustered Water™ is recommended.
- Fresh vegetables and green vegetable juices (try adding Granny Smith apples to juice for flavor)
- All fish except shellfish
- Free range or organic chicken and turkey
- Eggs
- Lemons, limes, Granny Smith apples
- Well-cooked millet, buckwheat, amaranth, quinoa, spelt, or teff
- Pasta made from any of the above recommended grains
- Essential fatty acids such as flax oil
- Clarified butter
- Raw almonds and seeds, raw almond butter
- Chamomile, peppermint, and Pau d'arco teas
- Green super foods such as Creation's Bounty®
- Stevia, a naturally sweet herb

AVOID THESE IF YOU THINK YOU HAVE PARASITES

- White potatoes
- Egg plant
- Tomatoes
- Red peppers
- High carbohydrate diets can make parasitic infections worse, so limit the carbs, and that includes breads.

- Be careful with the purity of your flour. If you knew the bugs and other stuff that makes their way into the flour you use, you would inspect it carefully.

- No matter what, always avoid water that may be infected. This includes tap water, well water, spring water, mountain water, etc. Remember, if you order drinks in a restaurant, the coffee, tea, and soft drinks probably are made using tap water and may contain these unwanted elements.

- Never eat raw or undercooked beef, pork, chicken, or fish. Shrimp alone can contain 60 types of parasites.

- Unwashed fruits or vegetables

- Water chestnuts and watercress

- Wheat

- Generally limit sugar intake: sucrose, fructose, maltose, lactose, glucose, mannitol, sorbitol, galactose, maple syrup, brown, raw, and date sugar, honey, and artificial sweeteners

- Alcohol, soda, coffee, fermented beverages, ciders

- Condiments, sauces, and vinegar products (mayonnaise, ketchup, MSG, pickles)

- Dried or candied fruits, such as raisins or dates

- Fermented foods such as soy sauce, tofu, tempeh, sauerkraut

- All fruit juices

- Fruits except those listed above.

- Cheese and sour milk products, buttermilk, sour cream

- Mushrooms

- All nuts except raw almonds and seeds

THE ONE PERFECT DIET—  THE LEVITICAL PLAN

DID YOU KNOW THAT GOD HAS PROVIDED A PLAN FOR EVERYTHING WE NEED, including what to eat to keep ourselves in vibrant health and with a strong immunity system that fights off parasites naturally? It's true, and God's plan is that we be submitted to Him in every area of our lives. He wants us to be free from other controls and dominion (Romans 6:14), including being in bondage to food. We've been redeemed from all bondages by the death and resurrection of Jesus Christ our Lord. I believe that He alone should have authority over our spirit, soul, and body.

We need to bring our eating under submission to God. We are spiritual beings who live in physical bodies. We are the temples of the Lord. Our body is merely a vehicle for fulfilling His purpose on the earth. Once you get that perspective, you'll eat to live, not live to eat. So before you read the following plan for eating God's way, take a moment to pray and submit yourself to God. Ask the Lord to show you areas where you can enhance your daily living by making dietary changes. He will show you, because He wants you to have victory in this area of your life.

GOD'S ANCIENT PLAN

God had a plan for healthy eating from the very beginning. Those who follow it walk in health, and those who don't are left to struggle with malnutrition, obesity, and disease. Need proof? Studies show that Israel is the healthiest nation on the earth, while the United States is ranked a dismal 96. That statistic alone should make you stop and take notice of what God has to say about your diet.

To fulfill the Word of God, the Jews observe the laws of Kashrut (keeping Kosher) as established in the Old Testament—what an awesome testimony of faithfulness and obedience to God! So many times we think of the Old Testament as a lot of do's and don'ts, but we fail to realize that God never does anything without a purpose. Those do's and don'ts have meaning! Although we will probably never know all the intricacies of the full benefits from eating God's way, I want to explore a few.

Hosea 4:6 says, "My people are destroyed from lack of knowledge." That's where most people stop reading. Let's finish the verse, though! God says, "Because you have rejected knowledge, I also reject you . . . because you have ignored the law of your God." Does that mean you're not going to heaven if you do not follow the dietary laws of the Old Testament? No, of course, not. The early church made it clear that it was not a mandatory part of the Christian faith (Acts 15). But I do believe that when we disregard the wisdom that God has already provided, we lose—in this case, our health.

Fad diets work temporarily, with an 85-percent failure rate of lasting weight loss. Starving works great until you start eating again. Exercise is fantastic, but if you don't eat right, your body will still starve for proper nutrition. This will absolutely show up in one manner or another. Everything in life is about choices, so set your will toward making right decisions and reap the wonderful rewards God has in store for you.

Psalm 103:1-5 says, "Praise the Lord, O my soul; all my inmost being, praise his holy name. Praise the Lord, O my soul, and forget not all his benefits—who forgives all your sins and heals all your diseases, who redeems your life from the pit and crowns you with love and compassion, *who satisfies your desires with good things so that your youth is renewed like the eagle's.*" So many times we only look at the fact that we want our youth renewed, and we overlook the prerequisite, which is satisfying our desires with good things. Not things that just taste good, but things that *are good* for us!

We can't separate the Word of God. For example, you may have heard someone quote, "Resist the devil, and he will flee from you" (James 4:7). That's not all that it says, though! The first half of the verse states, "Submit yourselves, then, to God." Depending upon what you quote, you get two totally different meanings. One in which you have no responsibility, and the other in which you must submit to God. We all need to submit to God's plan so that we can enjoy the true blessings of God, whether it is in spiritual warfare or in our eating. God's plan is that we treat our body as the temple of the Lord and feed it the right sustenance so that we walk in healing every day of our lives.

Blessings to all who endeavor to make lifestyle changes that will positively affect you in all you do.

KASHRUT TERMS

Kosher—properly prepared or ritually correct under Jewish law.

Milchik—food that is or contains milk or milk derivatives.

Fleischik—food that is or contains meat or meat derivatives.

Pareve—food that has none of the above properties (neutral foods such as fish, fruits, or vegetables).

KASHRUT PROCEDURES

Do not mix dairy and meat products. The traditional Jews will not even use the same dishes or cookware; much less eat them at the same meal.

Meat and fowl must be slaughtered correctly to be Kosher.

Fruits and vegetables are considered pareve (neutral) and may be served with either milk or meat foods.

Fish that has both fins and scales is considered Kosher and pareve. However, fish is not to be cooked together with meat.

FUNDAMENTAL RULES

■ Only the meat and milk of certain animals is permitted. This restriction includes the flesh, organs, eggs, and milk of the forbidden animals.

- Of the animals that may be eaten, the birds and mammals must be killed in accordance with the Jewish law.
- All blood must be drained from the meat or boiled out of it before it is eaten.
- Certain parts of permitted animals may not be eaten.
- Meat (the flesh of birds and mammals) cannot be eaten with or cooked with dairy. Fish, eggs, fruits, vegetables, and grains can be eaten with either meat or dairy. (According to some views, fish may not be eaten with meat.)
- Utensils that have come into contact with meat may not be used with dairy, and vice versa. Utensils that have come into contact with non-Kosher food may not be used with Kosher food. This applies only if the contact occurred while the food was hot.
- Grape products made by non-Jews may not be eaten.

According to Leviticus 11:3 and Deuteronomy 14:6, you may eat any animal that has cloven hooves and chews its cud. This includes cattle, sheep, goats, buffalo, and deer. It specifically excludes the hare, pig, camel, and the rock badger (you probably won't have a problem staying away from the latter two animals).

In Leviticus 11:9 and Deuteronomy 14:9, shellfish such as lobsters, oysters, shrimp, clams, and crabs are all forbidden. Fish such as tuna, carp, salmon, and herring are all permitted.

For birds there is less criteria. Leviticus 11:13-19 and Deuteronomy 14:11-18 list birds that are forbidden but does not specify why. However, they all are birds of prey and/or scavengers, which is why the rabbis said they were set apart. Birds such as chicken, geese, ducks, and turkeys are all permitted.

SOME EXAMPLES OF NON-KOSHER FOODS

Pork, rabbit, and horse meat; fowl, such as owl and stork; fish, such as catfish, eels, shellfish, shrimp, and octopus; and insects are all non-Kosher foods according to biblical definitions.

CAN PROCESSED FOOD BE NON-KOSHER?

Yes. This is because all ingredients and sub-units in a product must conform to the dietary laws in order for the food item to be considered Kosher. Even one non-Kosher ingredient can render the entire product unsuitable. Soda may contain a flavor enhancer called castorium, which is extracted from beavers. Cookies may contain a non-Kosher emulsifier, which is derived from animal fat. Potato chips may be fried in animal oil. So read your labels carefully.

The important point is not to get into the bondage of having to look for everything marked "Kosher," but to realize that God has given us a very clear plan for the foods we should eat. For example, the laws regarding Kosher slaughter are so sanitary that Kosher butchers and slaughterhouses have been exempted from many USDA regulations.

Non-Kosher slaughterhouses often operate in a manner far different from what God intended. I know this firsthand. My husband and I visited a non-Kosher slaughterhouse to see if we were interested in raising cattle on our farm. The butcher said, chuckling to himself, "If the cow wasn't fat enough when we brought it in, we put it out back and shoot it with a few hormones to increase its weight so we can get more money." We also inquired as to how the animals were butchered. He said, "We either shoot them or knock them out with a sledgehammer." That was enough information to make our decision. Those practices are far from God's plan!

In Kosher slaughtering the method is that of slicing the throat, which causes unconsciousness within two seconds, and is widely recognized as the most humane method of slaughter possible. There is no pain or fear in the animal, with no chemical releases, whether natural or synthetic. In this method, there is also rapid and complete draining of the blood. The Bible specifies that we do not eat blood because the life of the animal is contained in the blood. This is true even for an egg that contains a blood spot when cracked.

Today we know that disease is found in the blood, and if it is not drained properly, you can ingest it into your system. To show the comparison of Kosher to non-Kosher slaughtering, look at the contrast. In the typical meat plant, many animals are brought in at one time. The animals are lined up and either shot or hit with a sledgehammer. The animals experience fear brought on by the noise of the gun, the hammer, and the animals' cries of pain. When a mammal experiences fear, adrenaline is released into its bloodstream to help it flee. As the animal is slaughtered, these hormones are released into the bloodstream and then spill over into the flesh. The blood in the organs is also spilled into the flesh. What does this mean? It means that anything previously given to the animal, such as antibiotics, hormones, or even bacteria-laden feed, will now be ingested into you as you enjoy your steak dinner.

SEPARATION OF MEAT AND DAIRY

The Torah says that meat and dairy should never be consumed together. Spiritually, the Jews believe that it is callous to take an animal's life in order to satiate their own appetites. So they don't drink milk, which represents the nurturing of animal life, when they eat meat, which represents the destruction of life.

Once again, God had a dual purpose for a waiting time between eating meat and dairy. First, there is evidence that the combining of meat and dairy interferes with digestion. It's important to realize that the key to losing weight naturally and living healthy is dependent on good digestion and the absorption of nutrients. Whatever inhibits digestion needs to be avoided.

Plus, it is no coincidence that it takes approximately three hours to digest fish and fowl and anywhere from six to eight hours to digest meat. Why extend that time with milk? No modern food preparation technique can reproduce the health benefit of the Kosher law of eating them separately.

Remember that anything from an animal is high in fat, so eat more fowl and fish and less red meat. They take less time to digest, which means more energy for you and less energy devoted to processing a large piece of meat. Stick with Kosher if possible. If Kosher is not available, go for the hormone-free.

THE EXCELLENCE OF FISH

According to Leviticus 11:9, fish is considered to be a clean food. It is naturally low in calories and rich in health-giving oils as well as essential vitamins and minerals. Fish contain important Omega-3 fatty acids, which have been proven to lower cholesterol, inhibit blood clots, lower blood pressure, and reduce the risk of heart attack and stroke.

For years cod liver oil has been used as an immune system booster and tonic to cure any number of ills. Today, medical experts are seeing the wisdom that has been in God's plan from the beginning of time. Researchers at Rutgers University have shown that fish oil is also an effective cancer fighter, reducing your risk of breast, pancreatic, lung, prostate, and colon cancers. Migraine sufferers also find great relief with Omega-3 fish oils, according to studies at the University of Cincinnati. Another study there showed that people who suffer from psoriasis were helped tremendously after taking Omega-3 fatty acid.

The best fish sources, which are naturally low in calories, are salmon, mackerel, and halibut.

Shellfish and fish without scales are high in cholesterol and considered high-stress foods. Stay away from these. And stay away from fish that is not immediately put on ice—parasites that would be normally contained in discarded parts are allowed to travel up into the flesh where infestations occur.

TIPS ON EATING

- Before meals, eat 4 or 5 almonds. This will help to curb your appetite by sending a signal to the brain that you are full.

- A good oat bran is a great way to end your day instead of a heavy meal at dinner. A half-cup a day has also been proven to cut your risk of cancer by 30 percent. It is very effective in the elimination of waste from the bowels, acting like a broom that sweeps away the breeding ground of accumulated waste and disease. The bran fiber is an effective bulking agent that absorbs toxins and other wastes as it passes through.

- Wait 10-15 minutes before having a second helping. This is how long it takes to get the signal to the brain to tell you you're full. In doing this, you usually won't want a second helping.

- If you can avoid it, never eat past 6:00 p.m. in the evening! The later you eat, the less likely you are of burning it up. If you are having a smoothie, the time is not important because it is easily digested and absorbed.

- After your dinner, take a brisk walk. If your health does not allow it yet, start with walking in place for 5-10 minutes and increase as you can. If you're past that, go for it. Schedule in exercise three times a week. Remember there will never be a good time to exercise. You have to create one. At least 20-30 minutes is a good place to start. As with all changes in diet and exercise, consult with your physician first.

- Don't drink anything with your meals. If you must drink, have water with a slice of lemon. Sodas, teas, and coffees interfere with the stomach acids and enzymes vital for digestion.

- If you have a problem with poor digestion, try a glass of steam-distilled water with a teaspoon of raw honey, a fourth of a fresh lemon, and two tablespoons of organic apple-cider vinegar. This mixture can be taken with each meal and has been proven to increase your digestive ability. Many of those with chronic upset stomach, acid indigestion, and gaseous problems find themselves being relieved with this inexpensive home remedy.

- A study was done of men from all around the world. Surprisingly, the healthiest men over all were French! Considering the typical heavy, sauce-covered French foods, this fact is quite shocking. The three things that made the difference in their diet were the following: a little red wine, which aids in digestion; lots of fresh foods and fresh herbs; and, most important of all, they ate their salad last. The living enzymes in the fresh vegetable eaten last works to break down all the other foods just eaten. It is an excellent palate cleanser, and because of that, it helps you to make the right choice in not choosing a dessert. With all your food being broken down more efficiently, you get better absorption of all your nutrients, you feel better, and you have more energy. It is not abnormal to have your salad served last in a European country, so next time you're dining out, go the European way. Eat your salad last!

■ Remember: the ball of your fist is the size of your stomach when it is empty. Open up your palm. That should be the portion size you eat at each meal. More than that at a time, and you are overeating!

TIPS ON FOODS

■ Eat as many *fresh fruits and vegetables* a day as possible. By eating five per day, according to Johns Hopkins University, you can cut your risk of cancer by 30 percent and lower your systolic blood pressure by 5.5 points and the diastolic pressure by 3.0 points. Their researchers concluded that you could reduce your risk of heart disease by 15 percent and the risk of a stroke by 27 percent.

■ Researchers at Loma Linda University in California have shown scientifically that Kyolic® (a brand of garlic capsules found in any health food store) reduces the dangerous LDL levels of the blood and increases the beneficial HDL levels. A study in India showed that garlic has the ability to reduce blood clotting as well as serve as an anti-cancer agent.

■ Go to your local health food store and get a good powdered kelp to use for your seasoning. This is a great additive to your food as well as a plus to the thyroid, which controls your entire metabolism. A liquid bladder wrack—an old herbal remedy used for low thyroid—is also excellent when on a weight-loss program. It's very natural to the body and excellent for weight loss by speeding up the metabolism with no harmful side effects.

- A good rule of thumb is to stay away from processed foods. Then you don't have to be concerned about those hidden ingredients labeled as "natural flavoring." Try to eat foods that are as close to the way that God created them—chemical free!

- Water is vitally important to your body. Drink half your weight in ounces daily. Adding more water to your diet will make a big difference in your weight loss and health level, as well as change.

- Think about sprouting at home. It's easy, it's fun, it's cheap, and it tastes good! Even the kids love them and love to grow them! They're great on sandwiches and salads, and they can be used as snacks as well. The rewards are great. They are loaded with trace minerals that are not so easily found in other foods. You can get everything you need at your local health food store to sprout.

- Go for foods rich in color! Stay away from the white deadly things! White sugar, white flour, white salt, even white potatoes. Choose red potatoes instead of white. Choose a dark lettuce or spinach instead of iceberg.

- Go for Bible snacks instead of the processed foods. Fresh fruits, fresh veggies, nuts, raisins, granolas, yogurts, unrefined crackers, and flat breads—get creative! Genesis 43:11 specifically mentions pistachios and almonds. That's interesting in that those are particularly low in fat and calories. Nuts in general are a great snack food, with the exception of peanuts, which are really not a nut! Nuts are naturally rich in zinc, copper, iron, calcium, magnesium, and phosphorus, as well as being high in protein. Dr. Walter Troll of New York University says that nuts are among the top cancer-fighting foods in the world, containing cancer blockers. Nuts also help to keep blood sugar levels steady so you don't get those bothersome hunger pangs that can lead you to grab the first snack you can find, which is normally high in sugar and carbohydrates.

- Yogurt, or fermented milk, isn't mentioned in the Bible, but according to history we know that it was a mainstay at that time. Yogurt has been attributed to longevity in many civilizations. It is the ideal diet food for folks who want to add flavor and health benefits to their diet. Be sure not to get the yogurt with artificial sweeteners or with added sugars. Yogurt is a natural antibiotic that keeps your digestive system healthy by replacing the good flora in the intestinal track. This is needed for a healthy immune system. You can use yogurt in a variety of ways with salad dressings. It's a healthy snack—my favorite is my *Creation's Bounty* Shake with yogurt in the mornings! Those who are lactose-intolerant typically do fine with a good yogurt.

- Extra virgin olive oil is by far the best oil you can use! It has been proven to be the healthiest for your heart as well as lowering your cholesterol level instead of clogging your arteries the way the saturated fats found in your typical grocery store oils and margarinated butter does. It is far more versatile and can be used for just about anything. Medicinally speaking, olive oil has proven to be a natural antibiotic as well as antiviral. It tastes great and is good for you!

PRACTICAL APPLICATION

Putting the Levitical Diet into your daily living is actually very easy once you get in the swing of things. The important key is to get the body back into a place of homeostasis, which is a happy, healthy body, and the proper foods will make a world of difference. The rewards of healthy living, an energetic body, and sound, clear thinking will cause you to never want to turn back.

Remember that God's way works!

"Fruit trees of all kinds will grow on both banks of the river. Their leaves will not wither, nor will their fruit fail. Every month they will bear, because the water from the sanctuary flows to them. Their fruit will serve for food and their leaves for healing" (Ezekiel 47:12).

THREE POWER BOOSTERS TO YOUR IMMUNE SYSTEM

A WEAKENED IMMUNE SYSTEM IS AN OPEN DOOR THAT PARASITES ARE QUICK TO PASS THROUGH. The best security system that one can employ is to strengthen one's internal defenses to them. Unfortunately, parasites will never go away, thus our defenses can never be allowed to deteriorate.

Numerous factors have evolved that significantly contribute to a decline in our immune systems. Much has been written about the effects of pollution, pesticides, hormones, antibiotics, stress, poor diets, and the lack of proper supplementation for vitamins and minerals. On top of that many people fail to keep themselves fit, almost conceding themselves to a weakened condition that invites in disease and parasite infestations.

The Levitical Diet will go a long way to helping you restore your immune system to health as well as maintain it. Foods rich in vitamins and minerals and proteins and fiber give you more than a fighting chance against parasites. And it cuts down the dietary excesses and imbalances that most of us have allowed into our lives.

But it is also possible for individuals to be deficient in

single or multiple nutrients that need to be supplemented. You can indemnify the health of your immune system by the supplementation of vitamins and minerals and herbs that improve your immune function. I have three supplements in particular that I want to bring to your attention as true power boosters to your immune system.

THYMIC FORMULA

The thymus gland is a flat, pinkish-gray organ that plays an instrumental role in the immune system of our body. It is located high in the chest cavity behind the breastbone and extends into the lower neck below the thyroid gland. The thymus aids in the development of white blood cells called lymphocytes, which help the body fight diseases. Lymphocytes travel to the thymus, where they are changed into T cells by a substance produced by the thymus that is called thymosin. Those T cells leave the thymus and inhabit the blood, lymph nodes, and spleen. From there they attack bacteria, cancer cells, fungi, viruses, and other harmful organisms. T cells are sometimes called "killer cells" because of their ability to find and destroy such organisms.

God placed the thymus within us to defend against all these problems. I often compare it to the great walled cities in the Old Testament that were built to "keep the enemy out." They had huge fortified gates; some were even thick enough that they had apartments inside the walls. That's exactly what the thymus gland does for your immune system. When it is functioning properly you are living in a walled, fortified city that's going to protect you from the contaminates that we face every day.

But most of us are living in a city with holes in our walls. The walls are eroded and some of us even have our gates wide open with the doors knocked off, and the enemies are freely coming in and out. There's not even a guard at the door of our immune system to hinder invaders, whether it's parasites or hepatitis B, hepatitis C, rheumatoid arthritis, psoriasis, multiple sclerosis, or systemic lupus.

But remember, God has made provision for this. And here's where I want to tell you a amazing story that will give everyone hope.

I was first introduced to Dr. Carson Burgstiner and his work through a story that a medical correspondent reported on with the initial intention of exposing a medical "Quack." Dr. Burgstiner was a board certified OBGYN, a past president of the Medical Association of Georgia, a fellow of several very prestigious medical associations, and the subject of some amazing cures. And what began as a story described by a very suspicious reporter turned into a convincing picture of changed lives as patients were interviewed and their stories told.

Dr. Burgstiner had been forced into a non-surgical practice after accidentally pricking his finger and contracting the hepatitis B virus from a patient. This chronic and sometimes fatal form of hepatitis was unrelenting, and Dr. Burgstiner focused his attention on his body's inability to heal itself. He centered his attention on the thymus gland, and the fact that this gland can eventually stop functioning altogether as we move into adulthood. The person continues to live but without the benefits of the gland's support, although the lymph nodes and the spleen are supposed to be able to take over the task of producing lymphocytes.

He considered that when the thyroid gland slows or stops working, thyroid supplement is prescribed. And if the pancreas stops functioning, insulin is ordered, and so on. And so he began using thymus gland for his immune system. As the story goes, Burgstiner went to his health food store and purchased these extracts along with other vitamins and minerals that would support his endeavor, and six weeks later, after a seven-year battle his blood test for the hepatitis virus was negative. Not only did the independent lab find his sample negative, but also the Center for Disease Control in Atlanta, Massachusetts General Hospital in Boston, and the Scripps Institute of California, proclaiming him to have experienced a "spontaneous remission."

As Dr. Burgstiner treated other patients for various ailments, his years of experimentation and analysis identified a specific combination of nutrients, including extract of thymic glandular tissues that appeared to stimulate his patients' malfunctioning immune systems and reverse even supposedly incurable conditions. For the rest of his life he was dedicated to the research, refinement, and documentation of the near miraculous results that he and many of his patients experienced using this thymic protocol.

Independent laboratory tests prove that they created marked increases (up to 700 percent) in immune-system activity, as measured by the levels of thymic hormones in the blood. Further research demonstrates that the thymic extract alone, without the vitamin and mineral formula, did not have the same effect. Dr. Burgstiner theorized that the nutrients provided key activating agents for the natural synthesis of immune factors.

Dr. Burgstiner felt that his thymic formula produced an immune-regulating effect. That is, in hyper-immune conditions, such as rheumatoid arthritis and multiple sclerosis, it would turn the overactive immune response down. In hypo-immune conditions, such as cancer, it would turn the immune response up. His patients reported that, in general, they experienced a significant improvement within 30 days. So in a 30-day period you could begin experiencing, perhaps for the first time, the awesome power of a functional immune system. Naomi Judd was a patient of Dr. Burgstiner and used this formula and is now free from hepatitis C.

LACTOFERRIN

Lactoferrin is a type of cytokine—an immune chemical that helps coordinate the body's cellular immune response, defending against invaders such as bacteria and viruses that some parasitologists also classify as parasites. In particular, it functions as a type of border guard and shield against infection. This potent, natural immune booster has been reported to hinder tumor growth and metastasis, relieve the suffering of AIDS-related complexes, and protect the immunologically vulnerable from deadly viruses and bacterial infections. In healthy individuals, it can mean near-total immunity from colds, influenza, microbial parasites, and infectious bacteria. Its healing powers appear to be unrivaled. And yet, Lactoferrin remains largely unknown and poorly understood, even in the alternative medical community.

In a healthy individual, Lactoferrin is found in secretions such as tears, perspiration, the lining of the intestinal tract, and the mucous membranes that line the nose, ears, throat, and urinary tract—in short, any place that is especially vulnerable to infection. But by far the highest concentrations of Lactoferrin are found in a substance called colostrum (or "first milk"), produced by a new mother in the first few hours after she gives birth. For the newborn, Lactoferrin provides crucial immune-system stimulation, helping the new baby to survive in its new germ-laden environment outside the womb.

Recently, scientists have discovered that using Lactoferrin in the form of a nutritional supplement can significantly boost the immune system and greatly enhance the body's ability to withstand and recover from infection and other illness. Many Lactoferrin supplements are produced using bovine colostrums from cows that have not been fed antibiotics or hormones. The process used to create the commercial preparation leaves the Lactoferrin protein intact and chemically unaltered. (For those who are allergic to milk or lactose-intolerant, please note that the milk sugars responsible for lactose intolerance and the proteins responsible for cow milk allergies are largely absent in bovine colostrums.) Lactoferrin's actions extend far beyond the "cold and flu" season. Research has documented a long list of remarkable benefits, especially against retroviruses and malignancies. Lactoferrin can inhibit the growth of parasites, tumors, and metastasis, and scientists studying it report that it may be one of the best protective regimens against tumor formation.

You can't avoid exposure to parasites or the new "super cold" viruses or increasingly dangerous strains of the flu that appear each year, circling the globe with astonishing speed. But research indicates that Lactoferrin supplementation may be your key to developing an immune system that is strong enough to knock the bugs out before they take hold in your body. Lactoferrin increases both the number and the activity of at least a half-dozen different types of specific immune cells that help your body fight infection. The most distinguishing characteristic of Lactoferrin is its ability to bind to iron in the blood, denying tumor cells, bacteria, and viruses the iron they need to survive and multiply. But as researchers continue to test Lactoferrin against various disease processes, several more important functions have been revealed. The more Lactoferrin that is present in the body, the more effectively it performs its many immune-stimulating functions. There appears to be no toxic dosage, which is not surprising when you consider that high concentrations of Lactoferrin are well tolerated by newborn infants.

OLIVE LEAF

You may not believe it now, but infectious "smart bugs" are going to be the No. 1 threat to your health. In the past 15 years, death by infectious disease has already gone from being the fifth-leading killer in the United States to being the third-leading one.

Back in the golden age of antibiotics, doctors could destroy these disease-causing bugs with powerful drugs. But today, it doesn't seem to matter how quickly we invent drugs to kill them. Faster than we can create new antibiotics in our laboratories, deadly bacteria are developing resistance to the potent but limited drugs. There is one way, however, to stop these super-bugs. We can outsmart them, using the tremendous protective power of nature.

Nature's most promising antibiotic, antiviral, and antifungal agent is a compound derived from the olive leaf, called calcium elenolate. This plant extract not only helps your body battle the dangerous bugs that cause infectious disease, but also detoxifies your entire system, enhances your energy, improves your circulation, activates key components of your immune system, and has beneficial effects on cholesterol and blood-sugar levels.

Treatments made from the olive-leaf extract have been around for at least 150 years, with records dating back to 1827, when it was used as a treatment for malaria, which is a parasite, with no side effects other than those produced by the ethanol wine used in these special ethanolic preparations. In 1906, the olive-leaf extract was reportedly far superior to quinine for the treatment of malaria, but quinine, because it was easier to administer, became the treatment of choice. From 1970 to the present, a hydrolyzed form of oleuropein has been tested and found effective against dozens of different viruses and many strains of bacteria.

Now in capsule form, olive-leaf extract is making a comeback. Because it is a natural substance, olive-leaf extract has a much wider range of actions than man-made antibiotics. It contains a maze of chemicals harmless to us that lie in wait for invading bacteria. It directly stimulates phagocytosis—your immune system's ability to "eat" foreign microorganisms that don't belong in your body.

God's creation has provided germ killers far more potent than any that laboratory scientists can invent. The olive-leaf extract is one of these germ killers.

Thymic Formula, Lactoferrin, and Olive Leaf are all available from Valerie Saxion's Silver Creek Labs and listed in the back of this book.

CONCLUSION

DR. PETER WINA, CHIEF OF THE PATHO-BIOLOGY IN THE WALTER REED ARMY INSTITUTE OF RESEARCH, said, "We have a tremendous parasite problem right here in the U.S. It is just not being addressed."

My consultations consist mostly of individuals who have been to the best doctors, best hospitals, and had the best tests. They've had pills, shots, and surgeries, and many have the same comment: "I felt better for a while, and now I'm back to square one." Some of these same people also say, "You should see my cabinets. They're full of vitamins, minerals, and herbs. I've been to all the best alternative people, too, and I'm still in the same shape." And sadly a few will admit that someone has said to them, "It's all in your head."

There was a time in the United States when mothers dewormed their families as routinely as we still do our dogs, cats, and horses, but those days are long gone. And I believe the parasite problem is much worse than it was then because we travel more, eat more ethnic foods, have higher stress levels that inhibit our defense systems, and many engage in sexual promiscuity.

Aren't you amazed, after reading this, that you've never had a professional mention this information to you? That's what I hear all the time.

Parasite infestation isn't just a bad dream or nightmare. It is a reality, and I'm sure that by this point you are convinced of that.

Every Body has parasites, young and old alike, but I want to end with a special caution to seniors. The older a person is, the greater the chances are that that person's health is being negatively impacted by parasites and fecal backup. But the good news is that you can do something about this. If you follow the suggestions I've made, there's an excellent chance that you will be the next testimony of restoration. And I look forward to hearing from you.

If you write me with your specific testimony, I'll send you a free gift congratulating you for your efforts. Or just go on-line to Drval.TV, write your testimony, say you've read the book, and your gift will be on its way.

God bless you,

Valerie Saxion, N.D.
Silver Creek Labs
7000 Lake Country Drive, Suite C
Fort Worth, TX 76179-2900

TESTIMONIALS FROM CUSTOMERS

FROM THOSE WHO HAVE USED PARACEASE

"It has only been 10 days since I started the ParaCease program, and I wanted to share my progress with you. Just 10 days ago I:

- had an excessive appetite.
- was so bloated my husband said I looked pregnant!
- was overweight.
- was exhausted when I came home from work.
- had to nap before I could cook supper.
- hadn't slept well for years.
- and, I had no energy.

"Since I have a full-time job and four children, I thought most of this was normal. But as the Lord opened my eyes, I began using the information I heard you present on your program *On Call* on TBN and started the parasite cleanse. The first 3 days were a little difficult, but now what a difference! In just 10 days all the problems I mentioned above have vanished, and to top it all off I'm sleeping like I did when I was young. Dr. Val also suggested that I drink green tea and take some American Ginseng. I'm feeling great and don't even need a nap now before I cook. Who knows how good I'm going to feel after I've gotten rid of all these parasites."

—from a woman in Guadalupe, Texas

"Hello. I recently started using your products—Clustered Water, Body Oxygen, ParaCease, and Brain Sharpener. My eight-year-old son is using the Brain Sharpener, and I've already noticed a change after he took it five times! I have tried so many different supplements, hoping I would find one that could help his lack of focus. I praise God for these products. My husband thinks all these supplements do nothing, but when he started taking the ParaCease, he was blown away by how good he felt—not to mention what he saw come out. It's rather funny because six of us in the house are doing the ParaCease, and we're always asking each other what they have seen!

"When I spoke with your husband, he guided me in what supplements to take. He was very helpful. He also recommended to use a vitamin you don't sell. WOW!"

—Erin P.

"I am preparing to order my second month of the ParaCease products and am happy to say that I feel wonderful after using the product and changing my diet. My husband was totally skeptical of the whole procedure *until*

I saw my first 'critter' this week. Now he would also like to do the cleanse."

—J. Holbrook

"This testimony was received from a client I counseled and encouraged to use the ParaCease. She is 56 years young, but was very fatigued, overwhelmed, and constantly cranky. She committed to using the ParaCease for the full 90 days as recommended. She also followed the diet as closely as possible. After 90 days she was so excited and grateful. She lost 25 pounds, 3 dress sizes. She said her life was back in "balance." She was joyful and no longer plagued by food cravings. And she stated emphatically that she would continue to eat healthy and not allow the offending foods back to her diet."

—Melissa, C.H.

"A customer came in the office with complaints of pain, lethargy, and overall poor health and emotions for a prolonged period of time. After being on a parasite cleansing program, he came back with a jar of what appeared to be flukes that he had passed at home. He said he felt better after the huge purge, that his energy had returned, and that he was feeling positive and renewed. He decided to continue the cleanse for approximately 6 months to ensure complete cleansing."

—Rachel, H.T.

"Betty had been on the ParaCease for about a month and passed several parasites through her nose. In her

excitement, she decided to mail them in to the office as her own personal testimony. Since then she has been a regular customer and has a new lease on life—more energy and no constipation, bloating, or gas."
—Rachel, H.T.

"Over the years I have had many symptoms of both parasites and Candida infection, so in February of 2003 I decided to try Dr. Saxion's organ cleanse. After and during this process I experienced miraculous relief from the Candida and lost 12 pounds to boot. I have recently applied her suggestions and ParaCease cleanses for parasites and the colon. I have seen the evidence of these with both yeasts and parasites. A 4-inch roundworm was the most obvious. I now feel and sleep better *and have a decreased craving for carbs and sugars.* My family and I will continue to use Dr. Saxion's fasting and detoxing instructions as well as her products. I didn't know these things were possible. Thank you, Dr. Saxion."

"Initially I didn't believe in parasites because my doctor had never said anything to me about them. I was in denial that they would be in my body. But I thought that if they were, it would be better get them out, so I decided to begin a parasite cleanse. After about two weeks of faithful consumption of the ParaCease, I looked in the toilet and saw a white worm. Not only was I mentally relieved and shocked (in a good way), but also my physical problems *went away, disappeared, immediately.*

"Since the birth of my children five years ago, my menstrual cycle was irregular and unhealthy. After only a week it began to normalize with reduced cramping. I also had felt nauseated in the morning when I ate or even thought about eating, and now I can eat three meals a day with no problems. This has also caused me to evaluate my diet and adopt a positive life style change. I often wonder what kind of parasites my doctor has and doesn't know about."

—Karen, N.T.

"I took the ParaCease and didn't notice anything for several weeks. But now that I think about it, a morning cough started to disappear and I did experience a decrease in gas. I suppose it was so incremental that it didn't occur to me until now that it's all gone. Well, since I didn't see anything after bowel movements for almost a month, I thought I was parasite free. I did not realize that most parasites are microscopic, so I was probably passing them and didn't even know it. Anyhow, one night I had an unusual need to go and was surprised when I saw what looked like a spaghetti noodle in the stool. I almost flushed it, thinking that's what it was, but curiosity got the better of me. I took a coat hanger and removed it, put it in a jar with alcohol, and stared at it for a few days. I guess I was in denial. But the outcome has been terrific (no pun intended). All I can say is that I feel better than I have in years. I suppose I'm actually getting some of the nutrition that belongs to me now.

"Thanks, and God bless you, Dr. Val."

PARACEASE

ParaCease is a natural herbal supplement formulated to help rid the body of unwanted *Candida* and parasites. ParaCease contains 16 powerful natural compounds with anti-fungal and anti-parasitic properties. These herbs, minerals, and fatty acids have long been used to assist the body in maintaining internal health. A cleanse program with ParaCease combined with sensible diet changes will leave you feeling energized, rejuvenated, and healthy.

LACTOFERRIN

Lactoferrin is a type of cytokine—an immune chemical that helps coordinate the body's cellular immune response, defending against invaders such as bacteria and viruses. In the event of an invasion of microbes, your body increases production of lactoferrin, which is directly toxic to bacteria, yeast, and molds. It binds to iron in the blood, denying tumor cells, bacteria, and viruses the iron they need to survive and multiply.

COMPLETE THYMIC FORMULA®

This remarkable product contains a synergistic blend of herbs, essential vitamins, minerals and amino acids, thymic and other glandular extracts, antioxidants, enzymes, and whole food extracts that nourish and strengthen immune function. Combining cutting edge nutritional support with hormone replacement therapy for the thymus gland, it is perhaps the most comprehensive all natural dietary supplement available today.

OLIVE LEAF EXTRACT

For centuries the olive leaf has been used in traditional medicine as an antiseptic, anti-hypertensive, astringent, fever reducer, and for numerous other purposes. In 1962 an Italian researcher reported that oleuropein, a bitter gly-coside found abundantly in olive leaf, was able to lower blood pressure in mammals. This sparked further research, which proved olive leaf to be a potent anti-microbial as well as antibacterial and anti-viral. This investigation included viruses such as herpes, vaccinia, pseudorabies, Newcastle, Cossacloe A21, Monloney sarcoma, leukemia, influenza, and many more.

ABSOLUTE SILVER NASAL SPRAY

Most users describe this nasal spray as miraculous and life-changing and extraordinarily effective! No nasal burning, attacks infection, reduces swelling, and aids in fast healing.

AQUA FLORA

A state-of-the-art, high-potency homeopathic that successfully fights *Candida Albicans* in record time. Employs the same principle as all effective vaccines.

BIO DOPHILUS

These soil based organisms (SBO's) crowd out pathogens, thereby helping to balance the entire digestive system by lowering colonic pH and restoring proper bacterial balance. They assist in restoring the natural alkalinity of the blood by eliminating harmful acid wastes and help to balance the hormonal system by stabilizing blood sugar and restoring glandular integrity.

BODY OXYGEN

A pleasant-tasting nutritional supplement that is meticulously manufactured with cold pressed aloe vera. The aloe is used as a stabilized carrier for numerous nutritional constituents, including magnesium peroxide and pure anaerocidal oxygen, hawthorne berry, ginkgo biloba, ginseng, and St. John's Wort. It helps to naturally fight infections, inflammation, and degeneration by taking oxygen in at the cellular level. It also commonly helps in colon cleansing, regular elimination, and provides a feeling of increased energy and mental alertness.

BOVINE THYROID

A naturally safe way to boost your natural production of thyroxin without the risk of various side effects. The thyroid is responsible for everything from your metabolism to your sex drive. If you suspect you are among the one out of every four Americans who suffer from an under-active thyroid, consult your physician and consider this as a natural alternative.

BRAIN SHARPENER

The IQ-Maximizer, 100 percent natural and herbal. The student's best help for mental clarity, concentration, creativity, and optimum brain power. May restore normal brain function for attention deficit disorder, Alzheimer's, Parkinson's, and other neurological concerns. May reduce cortisol levels, which is one of the main causes of depression and a key to muscle building. May eliminate constipation and promote regular toxin excretion.

CALCIUM/MAGNESIUM

The USDA reports that 78 percent of adult women and 56 percent of adult men don't get enough calcium from their diets. The majority of teenagers are also lacking this vital nutrient. Our liquid Calcium/Magnesium is pleasant tasting and supplies the proper ratio designed for optimal absorption, essential for the support of healthy bones and teeth.

CANDICID FORTE

This product, with its powerful agents that contain liver and gastrointestinal herbs to maximize its performance, has been greatly improved by using more consistent extracts and the addition of both berberine sulfate and oregano extract.

CANDIDA CLEANSE

A decade in the coming, this is the most powerful natural agent I know of in the fight against *Candida*. It is specifically formulated for TOTAL *Candida* cleansing.

CHELATION SUPPOSITORY

Until now chelation could only be administered as a three-hour drip in a medical clinic. Now you enjoy the benefits in the privacy of your own home through this quick and convenient alternative to the I.V. treatment. Not recommended for use by persons with kidney disease or failure, or for those who are on blood thinners or taking more than one blood pressure medication.

CHINESE HERB STIMULATING SHAMPOO BY PETER LAMAS

All-natural and botanically rich stimulating shampoo empowered by 50 Chinese herbs. Gently removes hair follicle-blockage and debris that can slow growth and eventually cause premature hair loss. Helps alleviate dryness, flakes, and itching!

CLUSTERED WATER

Dr. Lorenzen's Clustered Water is probably the greatest breakthrough in health science product development in this century. Clustered Water, produced at home using one ounce of solution to one gallon of steam-distilled water, replenishes the most vital support for all cellular DNA and the 4,000 plus enzymes that are involved in every metabolic process in your body. Increases nutrient absorption by up to 600 percent, which means your vitamins and organic foods will deliver far more vital nutrients to your body. Replicates the powerful healing waters of the earth! Excellent for cleaning out lymphatic fluids!

COLLOIDAL MINERALS

These minerals are a concentrated liquid extracted from a very rare, ancient deposit of plant origin. Our special low-temperature processing makes these minerals available in a colloidal state with pure water. No synthetics, coloring, or preservatives are added. Mined from the richest source in the United States for over 70 years. We guarantee over 70 colloidal minerals in each serving.

COLLOIDAL SILVER

A universal germ killer and natural antibiotic. It has proven superior to every other silver because of its ultrafine particle size in a cubical shape, positively charged with 30 to 35 parts per million. It contains no salt, electrolytes, or binders with zero contamination. A partial list of bacteria/viruses tested and neutralized with Colloidal Silver in the laboratory were Lyme, Herpes, Legionnaire, Staphylococcus, Aureus, Salmonella, Choleraesuis, Streptococci, Warts, Pseudomonas, Aeruginosa, Neisseria Gonorrhea, Gardnerella Vaginalis, Gangrene, and Candida. Great for burns as well.

COLON CLEANSE

Super herbal cleanse for those times when your eliminative system is not what it should be. Also excellent to assist in detoxifying and cleansing your body.

CREATION'S BOUNTY

Simply the best, pleasant-tasting, green, whole, raw, organic food supplement available—a blend of whole, raw, organic herbs and grains, principally amaranth, brown rice, spirulina, and flaxseed. This combination of live foods with live enzymes assists your body in the digestion of foods void of enzymes. You will gain vital nutrients, protein, carbohydrates, and good fats to nourish your body and brain, resulting in extra energy and an immunity boost as well. It is a whole food, setting it apart from other green foods on the market.

DIGESTIVE ENZYMES

Digestion is the means by which food is broken down in order for the body to utilize it. If this process is inhibited for any reason, it may be necessary to take a supplement to ensure sufficient digestion. Bloating, belching, burning, or flatulence immediately after meals are common symptoms of low gastric acidity. So are indigestion, diarrhea, constipation, multiply food allergies, and nausea after taking supplements. Research has shown that the ingredients in our Digestive Enzymes have proven to be very effective in the first stages of (stomach) digestion.

FAT MAGNET

This revolutionary formula includes LipoSan Ultra brand Chitosan, which has three times more fat-absorbing activity than other Chitosan products. Fat Magnet possesses a positive charge that actually attracts negatively charged fat. This electrostatic process helps remove unwanted fat from the foods you eat and gently eliminates it from your system. Can be taken with meals, offering a convenient and effective way to meet your weight-loss goals.

4-WEIGHTLOSS

Reduce your appetite immediately without harmful stimulants. Speeds up metabolism. Lose fat from your stomach, chin, eyebrows, eyelids, thighs, hips, and buttocks. Won't raise your blood pressure. Also detoxifies the liver.

GREAT LEGS

Millions of Americans, mostly women, suffer with varicose or spider veins, leg swelling, and discomfort due to poor circulation caused by venous insufficiency. For years the French have used the Great Legs formula to increase blood flow to the legs and feet and to reduce the prominence of leg veins. All natural Great Legs contains a special plant extract, Ruscus aculeatus, that causes the smooth fibers of the veins to contract, allowing oxygenated, nutrient-rich blood to flow more freely to the lower extremities. With regular use, it can improve the look of your skin, reduce the prominence of varicose veins, curtail swelling, cramps, and tingling, and actually invigorate lower extremities so legs feel lighter and more energized.

HAPPY CAMPER

The original "feel good" formula that was one of the first all-natural herbal mood products to include Kava Kava and Passion Flower in a special blend that helps you relax and reduces anxiety. This sophisticated blend of select herbs will lift your spirit and improve your attitude and, unlike single-ingredient mood products, provides you with a true sense of well-being.

HYDROGEN PEROXIDE

Non-hazardous, food-grade, liquid oxygen used for a variety of purposes, including the famous "Oxygen Bath." Ask for our free booklet on H_2O_2.

HYDROGEN PEROXIDE GEL

Bad bacteria (anaerobic) can't live in the presence of oxygen, which is why hospitals around the world use hydrogen peroxide to clean and sterilize wounds in the prevention of infections. Our gel goes one step further by binding the peroxide to the area of treatment with pure glycerin, allowing the active ingredient the extra time it needs to work.

LIVER BALANCE PLUS

The liver processes 90 percent of what you take into your body and needs to be cleansed on a regular basis. It's like giving your car a tune-up. Suddenly you feel like you have a new car.

OXYGEN SUBLINGUAL SPRAY

A concentrated form of Body Oxygen™ that quickly delivers oxygen through the thin lining under your tongue. It is packaged as a convenient, easy-to-carry spray, delivering a powerful dose of oxygen that stimulates mental activity and invigorates your body while delivering numerous herbal benefits when you are "on the go."

PH STICKS

Knowing your PH level is imperative. Disease thrives in an acidic environment. By checking your PH on a regular basis, you can make the adjustments needed to bring your body up to a more alkaline state.

RADIANT-C FACE & BODY WASH BY PETER LAMAS

Packed with a highly potent 7 percent L-Ascorbic Vitamin C, Radiant C is designed to brighten, clarify, and retexturize aging skin. It delivers energy without irritating or dehydrating, gently loosens and removes makeup, dead skin cells, oils, and gives a mild lather that leaves you looking and feeling fresher from head to toe. Best of all, there are no harmful chemicals.

RICE PROTEIN VOLUMIZING SHAMPOO BY PETER LAMAS

Rice protein strengthens and expands the diameter of the hair shaft to create thicker, more luxurious hair.

SELENIUM FORTÉ

Selenium is a very important trace element that also functions as a powerful antioxidant. Recent research has shown that appropriate selenium intake is associated with optimum health.

SEVEN FLOWERS

Is high blood pressure a problem? You must try this all-natural product. "It's an absolute miracle," reports Evelyn Keen, commenting on the hundreds of customers she's had reporting on the awesome effects of Seven Flowers on people's blood pressure and mood improvements.

SOY BALANCING CONDITIONER BY PETER LAMAS

Soy-rich conditioner detangles and protects hair of every type, even hair that has been chemically treated.

SOY HYDRATING SHAMPOO BY PETER LAMAS

Nature's protein revitalizing shampoo designed to restore and strengthen chemically treated, dry, weak, or damaged hair.

SUPER FLEX BACK FORMULA

Reduces pain and inflammation! Contains Turmeric, ginger, and Protykin trans-reversatrol imperative for phytonutrients that inhibit the COX-2 enzyme. Also included in this unique blend is Boswellin, which is known to reduce inflammation, and Kava Kava and magnesium to relax back muscles and break the pain cycle. In addition, it contains MSM and Glucosamine to repair damaged connective tissue. The combination in Super Flex makes this product complete for back support and pain!

WHEAT GRASS DEEP CLEANSING SHAMPOO BY PETER LAMAS

A naturally effective, gentle cleanser that removes residue and debris without stripping out the moisture and vitality while keeping hair color looking vibrant. Gentle enough to use every day.

YOUR DAILY MULTI VITAMIN & MINERAL

An all-natural, food-based vitamin and mineral supplement without iron and copper. Contains the nutrients you need to survive in a toxic world that has been depleted by harmful chemical spraying and failure to rotate crops.

To contact Silver Creek Laboratories for a complete catalog and order form, call (817) 236-8557, or fax (817) 236-5411, or write us at 7000 Lake Country Dr., Fort Worth, TX 76179.

TELEPHONE CONSULTATIONS

For persons unable to see Dr. Saxion in her office in Ft. Worth, we offer telephone consultations. A telephone consultation can provide you with personalized advice and information concerning most health issues. Consultations can cover any subjects you choose, and you may ask her anything you wish.

Dr. Saxion treats all discussions with telephone consultation clients as confidential communications, unless you ask her to talk with someone else about it. Dr. Saxion will do her best to provide accurate information and useful counsel in a professional manner. For legal purposes, however, Dr. Saxion has not formally entered into a doctor-patient relationship but that of a coaching or educational relationship. Technically, what is provided to clients is health education and counseling rather than medical advice. In addition to providing you with as much insight as is possible from a naturopathic prospective, Dr. Saxion frequently refers clients to leading alternative MD's who may specialize in that client's health issue.

We offer telephone consultations Monday through Thursday, 9:00 a.m.—4 p.m. Central Time. Early morning or after hour consultations may be arranged. Consultations can be scheduled in increments of 15, 30, or 60 minutes. We require payment in advance for all individual consultations. Credit cards, checks, or money orders are preferred, but cash is also acceptable. We are not able to accept insurance. Please send your payment to:

Valerie Saxion, N.D.
Silver Creek Labs
7000 Lake Country Drive, Suite C
Fort Worth, TX 76179-2900

In order to arrange an appointment for the consultation, please call 817-236-8557 or e-mail valerie@doctor-val.com. You may also include proposed times with your payment. We will then contact you by phone or e-mail when possible to confirm a consultation time. Following the receipt of your payment, we will reconfirm and will provide the phone number for you to call. This will often be the office number, but not always. If you are unable to keep a scheduled consultation appointment, we request that you cancel by e-mail or by phone at least 24 hours in advance. Otherwise, you will be charged for the time scheduled.

*W*HEREVER SHE GOES, VALERIE SAXION constantly hears this complaint: "I can't remember when I last felt good. I'm exhausted and rundown. How can I start to feel good again?" This book is Saxion's response to that question, but it goes far beyond just feeling good. "So why don't you feel *great* all the time?" she asks. "Why are you willing to settle for less than 100 percent?" She then lays out a *Lifelong Plan for Unlimited Energy and Radiant Good Health* to help readers give their bodies the opportunity to start feeling great in four basic steps.

Specifically, Saxion guides her readers into an understanding of how their bodies work, how to stop eating junk food, and the importance of body oxygen, exercise, and water. *Candida*, detoxification, fasting, low thyroid, and weight loss are all covered as well as establishing a perfect diet that is filled with foods that supercharge the mind and body. Nature's prescriptions of vitamins, minerals, and herbs supplement all that she teaches.

Includes a state-by-state list of more than 800 of America's leading complementary alternative medical doctors.

IF YOU'VE BEEN LOOKING FOR AN EXERCISE SYSTEM that will give you the results you've always dreamed of having, does not require either a gym or expensive exercise equipment, can be done anytime and anyplace without requiring an outrageous commitment of time, you're holding it in your hands.

Based solidly upon the most effective exercise systems as taught by Earle E. Liederman and Charles Atlas during the 1920s, *Pushing Yourself to Power* provides you with everything you need to know to help your body achieve its natural, God-given strength and fitness potential. Whether your desire is simply to slim down and shape up, or to build your maximum all-around functional strength, athletic fitness, and *natural* muscularity, you will find complete training strategies specifically tailored to the achievement of your personal goals.

Profusely illustrated with 100s of clear, detailed photos showing every facet of every exercise, you'll never have to guess if you're doing it right again. You'll achieve the stamina you've always wanted in less time than it requires to drive to a gym and change into exercise clothes. Feel what it's like to have twice as much energy as you ever thought you'd have!

The **Ultimate** Do It Now
Do It Anywhere
Lambs to Lions
Complete Guide to Total Body
Transformation

PUSHING YOURSELF to POWER

JOHN e. PETERSON

Unleash Your Greatness

AT BRONZE BOW PUBLISHING WE ARE COMMITTED to helping you achieve your ultimate potential in functional athletic strength, fitness, natural muscular development, and all-around superb health and youthfulness.

Our books, videos, newsletters, Web sites, and training seminars will bring you the very latest in scientifically validated information that has been carefully extracted and compiled from leading scientific, medical, health, nutritional, and fitness journals worldwide.

Our goal is to empower you! To arm you with the best possible knowledge in all facets of strength and personal development so that you can make the right choices that are appropriate for *you*.

Now, as always, **the difference between greatness and mediocrity** begins with a choice. It is said that knowledge is power. But that statement is a half truth. Knowledge is power only when it has been tested, proven, and applied to your life. At that point knowledge becomes wisdom, and in wisdom there truly is *power*. The power to help you choose wisely.

So join us as we bring you the finest in health-building information and natural strength-training strategies to help you reach your ultimate potential.

FOR INFORMATION ON ALL OUR EXCITING NEW SPORTS AND FITNESS PRODUCTS, CONTACT:

Strength & Honor

BRONZE BOW PUB

BRONZE BOW PUBLISHING
2600 East 26th Street
Minneapolis, MN 55406

WEB SITES
www.bronzebowpublishing.com
www.masterlevelfitness.com

612.724.8200   Toll Free **866.724.8200**   FAX **612.724.8995**